THE
SHADOW
CHILD

Living with a Sibling's Addiction

by Ashleigh Nowakowski

PathBinder Publishing

COLUMBUS,
INDIANA

Published by PathBinder Publishing
P.O. Box 2611
Columbus, IN 47202
www.PathBinderPublishing.com

Edited by Lori Haggard
Covers designed by Anna Perlich
Cover photo by iStock

First published in 2022
Manufactured in the United States

ISBN: 978-1-955088-18-3
Library of Congress Control Number: 2021924627

To my parents, Rick and Sandi, who have sacrificed so much for my brother and me; my husband, Ryan, who stood by me no matter what was thrown at us; my children, Nolan, Teagan, and Tenley, for giving me the strength to continue on through the tough days; my counselor, Roxanne, for helping me do the work; my friends, who have supported me; and to all those who have been or are affected by substance use.

Table of Contents

Foreword

*"This is Tom Farley, brother of Chris Farley,
who died of a drug overdose in 1997."*

For almost 25 years, that is how I have been described in articles and introduced at events or in media interviews. Even when people leave out the "who died of a drug overdose" part, I was forever being linked to my brother.

Almost immediately after Chris's death at age 33, I knew that I wanted to make a difference in the fight against substance abuse. So I started The Chris Farley Foundation and went into schools to deliver my message. I also wrote a New York Times bestselling biography, *The Chris Farley Show*, which honestly told his story and struggles with addiction. I was simply doing what I thought Chris would do, what we were both raised to do, which was to help others.

In the beginning the work I was doing served two purposes. At first, I sought to somehow manage my grief (and perhaps my guilt) after his death. I also wanted to do what I could to help manage Chris's legacy. For all the wonderful things I heard about my brother in the days after he passed away, I heard just as many words that were hurtful, insensitive, and judgmental.

There was, and still is, so much stigma associated with addiction and especially around someone who dies from drug use. So I leaned into this work to prevent substance abuse, to reduce stigma associated with this disease and to help others who share the pain of losing a loved one. And perhaps one day

I will be introduced as just "Chris Farley's brother" or, if I'm lucky, as simply "Tom Farley."

Which brings me to this wonderful and powerful book.

I met Ashleigh fairly recently, as our work in substance abuse prevention and treatment brought us together. The connection and common bond was immediately evident. Our stories were so very similar — a younger sibling who struggled with addiction, how we chose to deal with that experience, even choosing to write a book on the subject.

Like me, Ashleigh comes from a wonderful, close and caring family. And, like the Farleys, they were a group that liked to have fun. Her family has a positive infectiousness that effortlessly draws people together. Very Wisconsin!

I noticed something else that Ashleigh and I shared. We were two fairly introverted people who were forced by our circumstances to exhibit extroverted behavior. It's not a natural state of being for us. And there's probably a number of reasons why we embraced this path. It may have been to shield ourselves from the devastation that addiction had brought into our lives. Or we felt we needed to deflect attention from our sibling's struggles (sometimes driven by embarrassment, sometimes by concern). For whatever reason, we chose to dedicate ourselves to helping (or preventing) others from the devastation this disease creates. We became extroverts. And we became experts in a field we never imagined, or wanted, to find ourselves.

But here is where Ashleigh and I begin to differ. All these years, I have held back or ignored all the pain this experience has caused me. I thought that by dedicating myself to substance abuse prevention and treatment, I could ease that pain. To be out there advocating and speaking to multitudes of people was clearly helping others. But it was just a Band-Aid for me. And truthfully, I'm not sure I was truly even aware of this. I guess I just didn't want to go there. Thankfully I had a friend who did "go there."

Ashleigh took that brave step to honestly write about her story and how this disease personally affected her. The courage to speak about herself, her family, and her relationships is impactful enough. But to share her story with such openness and clarity demonstrates a vulnerability that few people can muster. And that alone makes this book unique.

In addition, what also makes this book important is everything that Ashleigh leaves us with. She does more here than bare her feelings. This book does not just describe the rollercoaster we go through when we are touched by a loved one with an addictive disease. No, Ashleigh has also done the work and all the heavy lifting that follows. She leaves us with tools we need to actually heal, to finally become that person we've hidden for so long.

I'm honored to have been asked to write this foreword, not just because of how I feel about this wonderful family or the bond of similar experiences we share. I write this foreword because I read this book and am truly grateful that I did. I connected to the "rollercoaster" and certainly related to the family dynamics Ashleigh describes. And of course, our work in substance abuse prevention was another bond we shared.

Her need to dedicate herself to work in the field of substance abuse prevention definitely resonated with me. But as Ashleigh began to explore her world as a "shadow child," I began to see myself there, as well.

I was not prepared for such recognition or the emotions it uncovered. Throughout my journey, there were many times that I, too, have felt pushed aside or "into the shadows" due to circumstances outside of my control. But if I'm honest, there were definitely times when I've retreated into those shadows on my own. Either way, it's not a great place to be, and it's certainly not a healthy place to be.

There are many siblings out there like Ashleigh and me, who feel we've been relegated to a life in the shadows. That is one of the many dysfunctions this disease creates. Thank you, Ashleigh, for letting us hear your voice and for finally showing us a way out of those shadows.

— Tom Farley

Introduction

Before you dive into this book, there are a few things I would like to make clear. First, perception is everything. The way that situations happened and the events that occurred in this book can all be perceived in different ways. This book is about my perception of how things happened and the events that took place. It is very one-sided — *my* side.

Second, I do not view myself as the victim. The only true victim is my brother, who is trapped deep inside his addiction and can't find his way out.

Third, the names and places have been changed to protect the identities of people. This book is about me, not my brother. Therefore, I give you the cast of characters in this book:

Sandi — Mother
Rick — Father
Travis — Brother
Karen — Travis's wife
Cindy — Mother of Kasen
Kasen — Cindy and Travis's son
Maggie — Travis and Karen's daughter
Ryan — Ashleigh's husband
Nolan — Ashleigh and Ryan's first-born
Teagan — Ashleigh and Ryan's second-born
Tenley — Ashleigh and Ryan's third-born
Roxanne — Ashleigh's counselor

Last, in no way, shape, or form do I blame either of my parents for the events that took place. Having a child with an addiction and mental health problems does not come with a manual. They did the best they could with the knowledge they had.

It is my greatest hope that sharing my thoughts, feelings, perceptions, and the things I learned along the way through my brother's addiction will bring someone in a similar situation some relief knowing that they are not alone, and the understanding that they don't have to be defined by someone else's addiction.

I have spent the last twenty-five years in the shadows beneath his use, his recovery, and his relapse. I have spent the last two years climbing my way out. This book is about finding myself and about all the pain, sadness, hurt, betrayal, anger, love, and happiness that come along with addiction.

Beginning

This section is short and to the point in order to provide a basis for my perspective a little later on.

I was born in January 1984 in Milwaukee, Wisconsin. Almost three years later, my brother, Travis, was born in December 1986.

My mom and biological father divorced when I was six and Travis was only three. Our biological father never played a role in our lives. He would show up every once in a while, then one day he vanished, abandoning us. I'm not even sure Travis would remember him at all. Our mom, Sandi, married Rick three years after her divorce. Rick took the role of father in our lives, and we were eager to call him Dad. Shortly after they married, we built a new house and moved an hour away. I entered our new school in fourth grade and Travis in first grade. Travis didn't seem fazed at all.

Our childhood was pretty average. Our dad owned his own landscaping business and worked all the time. Our mom quit her job after we moved and became a stay-at-home mom. She would drive us to school so we didn't have to take the bus, drive us to all of our sports events, and was always there whenever we needed something.

Travis and I both played soccer in our younger years. I started riding horses when I was twelve, and Travis switched from soccer to football. We didn't go on elaborate vacations or have fancy things, but we were comfortable. Every summer my parents would ship us off to Florida to spend three to four weeks with our grandparents. We would go boating, play at the beach, and dine in at the movies. I have such fond memories of our trips to Florida.

Travis was always a hyper child, but I never really noticed because I was happy to always have someone to play with. We were best friends. We spent our free time playing soccer in the yard, playing Nintendo, and he even played house with me.

In third grade, Travis was diagnosed with ADHD, and my parents reluctantly gave him medication. At the time, ADHD medication was fairly new, and they were afraid he'd lose his funny, bubbly personality. However, the medication did help, and he started doing better in school. He was always happy and so much fun to be around.

I, myself, have very opposite traits. I'm shy, introverted, and always follow the rules. Because I was the oldest and well behaved, I was given a lot of freedom. My parents trusted that I was doing what I said I was going to do, and I was always home on time. This led to Travis being given the same freedoms I had. And this is where the problems began.

Travis was allowed to walk to friends' houses after school and hang out until he went to football practice. We didn't find out until much later, but Travis began drinking and smoking cigarettes at the age of eleven with his friends' older siblings.

Some people begin experimenting with drugs or alcohol out of curiosity, depression, anxiety, rebellion, a prescription from a doctor, or just simply to fit in with others around them. This is where my brother's journey started. He had a need to fit in.

In middle school, Travis was chunky and people picked on him. Although I don't recall, I'm sure (being his older sister) I probably made comments as well. He wanted to fit in, and he truly felt that by drinking and smoking cigarettes, people were going to like him. And they did. He progressed to smoking marijuana in seventh grade.

Throughout middle school, our relationship remained strong. I had no idea at the time that he was using substances.

I was super naive to drug and alcohol use. Sure my parents drank, but I didn't know anyone in my middle school who drank alcohol or smoked cigarettes, and I knew nothing about marijuana, cocaine, heroin, or any other substances besides the little information we learned in D.A.R.E.

I never thought anyone in our area, let alone a middle school student, would use a substance. I was such a rule follower that I couldn't fathom someone breaking the rules like that. I'm sure my naivety about substances played a role in not knowing exactly what Travis was doing, but Travis hid it very well.

Things really started to change when he hit high school. He went from a tiny middle school class of thirty to a freshman class of six hundred. There were so many more kids that liked to drink, use drugs, and party — the very things he liked to do. And he was introduced to prescription pills.

As Travis started hanging out with these new friends, he began to give up things he loved. He no longer played football and always had "something to do." I know now that "something" was drinking or using drugs.

When I figured out that Travis was using substances, I honestly thought it was just a phase. Being three years older than him, I saw people in high school drinking or smoking cigarettes, and I thought it was normal. Doesn't every teenage kid experiment? But I also didn't know a lot about substances or addiction.

Eventually, he started skipping school. Where he went and what he did is still a mystery to me. He missed so much school that my mom got pulled into court. When the judge called her up for the truancy hearing, she asked the judge what she was supposed to do.

She dropped him off every morning and picked him up every day after school. She had no idea he was skipping class. This was around twenty years ago when we didn't have online access to attendance records. If she wanted to know whether or not he was absent, she would have had to call every day to see if he made it to class.

As time went on, things started to change. *He* started to change. He went from a fun, kind, hyper kid, to an angry, disrespectful little punk. I cannot pinpoint an exact time or event where I noticed the change; it was gradual. Things would be normal for a few days, then he'd be different. Then the "normal" times became less and less, and the not-so-nice times became more and more.

There were times when he would have so much rage because he didn't get what he wanted, usually money, that he would punch holes in the walls. At that point, I (and I think my parents as well) became afraid of him. He had started to become physical. We didn't know if that physical aggression would ever turn on us. Thankfully, it never did.

Most of the time we didn't know what mood he would be in. Is he happy today? Angry? Tired? It was much easier to move around the house when he was sleeping so we wouldn't have to face him. When we did run into him, his response to a simple *hi* would tell us everything we needed to know.

There were days when he was his old self, and I think that gave us all hope that things weren't as bad as we feared they were. Yet deep down inside we knew it would be short-lived, and the next day or the day after, he would be back to his punk ways.

As Travis started to change, so did my parents. They fought more, my mom cried a lot, and everyone was always walking on eggshells. They didn't know what to do or how to help him. During the time of his using, no one in the community was talking about substance abuse. If we did try to talk about it, people would look at us like we had a contagious disease that, somehow, they could catch, so no one wanted to be around us.

While my mom was sad about the situation, my dad was angry. Angry because, as a dad, he was unable to fix it. In his mind, he was supposed to be the one to help and make it all better, but nothing he did made the situation any better, and often it would get worse.

My dad, Rick, was born and raised up north in Wisconsin and still owned property up there. My parents even owned the local bar and restaurant that they had someone else managing for them. In an effort to try to help Travis overcome his delinquent ways, my mom, dad, and brother moved up north so he could finish school up there.

I was eighteen at the time, but I still had a few months of high school left, so I stayed behind. When they decided to move, leaving me all alone, I was relieved. For the first time in a long time I didn't have to see my brother's addiction. I didn't have to hear my mom's cries or my parents fighting. I was truly alone. Some people may think, *oh they abandoned her!* But, in all honesty, I was abandoned long before anyone left. I was so deep in the shadows — my brother the main focus — that when they left, I was able to come into the light. I started to gain a different type of independence. I had been operating on my own for a while, but now, with no one around, there was no more walking on eggshells. I was free to do what I pleased when and where I wanted to.

While up north, Travis joined the football team and seemed to be doing well. My parents thought the change in scenery and new friends were helping. But if there is a will, there is a way. He started stealing alcohol from the bar and found people who had drugs. Once that school year was over, they all came back home.

Next, my parents decided to move him to a private school close by. That lasted a week. I kid you not. The school called one week later and said, "Here is your check back with a full refund, your son is no longer welcome at this school." I don't know what happened during that week, but it must not have been good.

With nowhere to turn, my parents did what all struggling parents would do: they pulled out the phone book and looked for a counselor in our area. At this point Travis was about fifteen years old, and we didn't know the extent of his use. We just knew that he must be using some type of substance. We would always check his room for drugs, but we never actually saw the drugs. Once my parents found a counselor that would see him, they would take him to his appointments. He would come out and say he was doing great, and my parents would believe him. Six months later, when he was sick of that counselor (probably because they were no longer buying his bullshit), they would seek out a new counselor and start the process over again.

I, on the other hand, would get fed up with the cycle and repeatedly tell my parents something needs to change. "You have to be stricter," or "Take away his phone," or "Stop letting him leave with his friends and actually follow through on your consequences." My parents would give him a consequence like, "You're grounded for two weeks; you can't leave this house." Travis would be good for the first week, then my parents would give into his pleas and let him off the hook early. Though I could clearly see his manipulation, my parents were too close to it to see. They wouldn't listen to me. Afterall, what does a teenage girl know about parenting?

He ended up returning to his original high school and was placed in the alternative education program. In that program, they were only required to attend school for three hours a day. All his old, drug-using friends were in the same class. To me, it didn't seem fair because he caused trouble and only went to school for three hours, while I had to sit through eight hours of class time. I suppose they had their reasons. He ended up graduating with a high school equivalency diploma.

Because he was so irresponsible, my parents wouldn't allow Travis to get his driver's license. That didn't stop him from driving. He would drive his friends' cars. At the age of seventeen, he received the first of his three DUIs, the second two of which came after he got a driver's license. He also switched from using prescription pills to using heroin.

When I think back to this time period now, there was no clear indication of when he switched substances. I never saw a shift in his personality — he was always all over the place with his emotions, always had something to do, and always needed money whether he was drinking, smoking, or snorting heroin.

It came to the point where I began to hate my brother. I hated him for my parents fighting all the time, my mom crying every day, and the worry we felt that we would get that phone call that he wasn't coming home. I also hated that he didn't care. I couldn't fathom how someone could visibly watch their family falling apart because of their actions and not care at all. But, again, I didn't understand addiction.

Through all this, I felt this need to be perfect. Maybe it's just my type-A personality, but with everyone walking on eggshells at home, I never wanted to make any waves. If I had any problems or struggles, I never talked to my parents about them because they had enough going on. Actually, I didn't talk to anyone about them because I didn't think anyone would understand. We had been living this way for so long that it just became our "normal" family life.

I always had this fear that if I went to the guidance counselor at school and explained to them what was happening in my home, the problem would get worse. My parents would fight more because people knew what was going on, or the opposite would happen — no one would care, nothing would change. It was much easier to pretend like nothing was happening, so I felt very alone. There was no one I could talk to who would say, *I know exactly what you're going through.* I buried everything deep down inside and continued with my life like nothing was wrong. Even now, I keep a lot of it buried. I don't want to go back to that place.

Yet, through it all, I kept my grades up and spent most of my time at work or the horse barn so I didn't have to be around the drama. My brother always liked to throw it in my face that I was the "perfect child" and our parents gave me everything and him nothing. In reality, it was the other way around. All their time and energy were devoted to him. It didn't matter where we were or what we were doing, my parents were always thinking and worrying about Travis. Travis was always in the spotlight, me in the shadows.

During all of this, I was going through my own teenage "phases." I was trying to navigate life, figure out who I wanted to be, and decide where I wanted to go to school. I felt neglected by my parents because they were constantly focused on him.

Now, I was a straight-A student, had a job, and rode horses, so on the outside, I seemed to be doing well. But, deep within, I felt alone. My parents would physically be at my horse shows, but mentally and emotionally they were with my brother. I felt like I had to grow up on my own.

When I look back at that time period now, twenty-plus years ago, I don't know that I could have actually vocalized, or even identified, the feelings I had. Back then, I didn't know any different. It was just how my family operated. It wasn't until after my brother got sober and I learned about addiction that I could look back and identify those feelings.

At the age of sixteen, I lost my best friend in a drunk driving accident. That was a huge moment in my life. I learned that drinking and using drugs weren't worth it to me. I saw firsthand the pain her family went through. That kind of loss is a "physical" pain — a pain that hurts every single part of your body. If you've ever lost someone close to you, or even a pet, you know what I'm talking about. I didn't want to put my family through that. Little did I know that, years later, I'd be living through my own pain of my brother's addiction.

When I work with students who have similar stories to mine, I learn that some turn to drugs, drinking, cutting, or extreme rebellion and so forth to get their parents' attention. As for me, I looked for attention elsewhere.

It was the summer before my junior year of high school. I had just finished horse showing all day. I was exhausted but also sixteen and wanted to hang out with my friends. So I headed downtown to the local street dance. That night I met a boy — a boy two years younger than me that went to a different high school. And he was good looking. We hung out all night. We started dating shortly afterwards.

Since he obviously didn't have his driver's license, I did all the driving. I spent every available free moment I had with him. I had a good relationship with his parents and spent as much time at their house as I could because I did not want to be at home. I even ended up living with them for a time. *I really didn't want to be at home.* We were young and in love. We had our ups and downs, of course, but we ended up dating for five years.

When I think back to that time period now, I feel like I was looking for him to fill the void I had with my parents and my brother. This void had probably always been there since the day my biological dad left us. Add to it the loss of my brother to his addiction and my parents being so focused on my brother, and the hole grew wider. Every person in my life that I had known and trusted had left me — maybe not physically, but emotionally.

Because I was afraid to lose my boyfriend, I put so much into that relationship. But I lost myself. I gave up riding horses, I was only friends with his friends, and my whole life revolved around him and what he wanted. When I graduated high school, I was looking at colleges. Since my boyfriend was used to me being devoted to him and his needs, he hated the idea of me leaving. I was afraid of losing him, the only person I had in my life that I thought cared about me, so I never left.

Instead of going to college, I decided to move out of the house and into my first apartment with my boyfriend. We still had a pretty rocky relationship, but, for the first time ever, I had a place of my own. I didn't have to walk on eggshells or worry about getting lost in the shadow of my brother's addiction every day.

After high school, Travis got his driver's license started working in Dad's landscaping business. It's crazy to think now, but Travis could get up every day, go to work, then after work he would disappear for a while to find and use drugs, and then do it all again the next day. We knew that he was using something, but we didn't know whether it was alcohol, marijuana, pills, or some other substance. He was an adult now, and we had no idea of the extent of his use.

My dad has four older sisters who have a different father. Their father was killed while working on the railroad. Then his mom married Dick, and they had two sons. From the stories I've heard, Dick was an abusive alcoholic. He was very controlling, and if you didn't do what he wanted you to do correctly, there was hell to pay. I remember my dad telling me a story of when he was twelve and brought home a stray dog. Well Dick didn't want a dog, so he shot it right in front of my dad. That was the type of man Dick was.

Growing up in that environment, my dad thought he knew everything about addiction, but, in reality, he knew very little. And, like they always say, the apple doesn't fall far from the tree. Dad tried to control everything thinking that, if he maintained full control of everyone, the madness would stop. But it didn't. It just made Travis rebel even more. Thankfully, my dad isn't a drinker because that would have made the situation ten times worse.

For as long as I can remember, holidays and birthdays were always very special in our household. During Christmastime, my mom spent weeks decorating the house, picking out the perfect presents, and planning the perfect meal. For our birthdays, she made sure we had the best cake, tons of presents, and whatever we wanted for dinner.

But, eventually, holidays started to suck. It always seemed that something would happen on those days — nothing major, but little things. We would plan the celebrations, get excited, and then *bam!* — Travis would go missing or be high or start a huge fight. We started dreading holidays, always anticipating something would happen. There was never a major blow-up or event that made us feel this way. It just seemed like things gradually started changing. Mom would withdraw because it was supposed to be a happy day, but she knew her son wasn't 100%. Dad would be on edge and crabby because Mom was withdrawn. It's hard to put into words the weight that hung in the air. Once the holiday was over, we were all able to breathe again. To this day, I don't know why we thought our holidays had to be perfect, but it was an expectation we set for ourselves that we just couldn't shake.

When Travis was eighteen, he met a girl named Molly. Molly was sweet and kind, and I thought maybe she'd be able to settle Travis down or whip him into shape. Maybe he would stay home more, be less impulsive and less angry. Maybe she would be the one that he would stop using drugs for. I didn't spend much time with them, so I don't know if she knew about Travis's use, whether she cared, or if she used, too. Six months into their relationship, she became pregnant.

My parents and I were happy, hoping this was it. Bringing a baby into this world would be his wake-up call that he needed to stop all his shenanigans. Yet we were also worried because we didn't know if he was ready to take on the commitment of taking care of a child.

Five months into her pregnancy, Molly went into early labor which the doctors could not stop. The baby was born lifeless. When Travis called me from the hospital at 2 a.m., I hopped out of bed and drove to the hospital. I walked into the room and saw my brother holding his little boy, his world shattered.

Three days later, we held a funeral for the baby. When the casket was laid to rest in the ground, my whole family cried — not only for the loss of the child, but for the fear that we would be burying my brother next. We knew that this tragedy would not stop him from using drugs. In fact, we knew it would only escalate his use. Was he so hurt by his loss that he would end his own life? Would he just give up and succumb even further to his addiction? Or would this be the turning point for him? We had all these questions, but, based on Travis's past, we knew he would refuse help and continue using. This is exactly what he did.

The weeks following the delivery and the funeral were some of the scariest. We knew that Travis was suffering. We also knew that he was using substances to cope and refusing to see a therapist.

At this point, his life really started to spiral. He received his second DUI and spent time in jail for driving without a license. We rarely saw him except when he'd show up for work when he needed money or when he needed a place to sleep for a few days.

Around this time, after two years of living with my boyfriend,

I decided to end things. There wasn't a major fight; nothing happened to make me leave. My boyfriend and his dad had gone to Florida to help with the clean-up after a major hurricane, and, for the first time ever, I was alone. I didn't need to take care of him, entertain his friends, or wait on him hand and foot. Although it was scary to be alone, it made me realize that I *could* be alone, that I didn't *need* someone. So I decided to walk away.

I learned a lot from that relationship. For five years, I thought I needed my boyfriend to make me feel whole, to make me happy. The truth was I *wasn't* happy, and that relationship didn't fill the hole I had; it only masked it.

Even being away from my family and living on my own didn't wntirely free me from my brother's addiction. Travis would still call me to ask to hang out at my place, give him a ride, or pick him up from jail. I'd also hear about his shenanigans from my mom. Still, it was a decent break — until I moved back in with my parents.

By now my brother's addiction was so rampant it was almost unbearable to be in the house. I remember one specific night where he "borrowed" my mom's car and never came home that night. Two days later, he showed up with the car smashed on one side. He said he hit a guardrail going a hundred miles per hour. Whether that was true or not, this had become our lives. Nothing shocked us anymore. Yet we still had no idea how to change it.

Throughout these years, I would always say to my parents, "You have to do something different! Kick him out, call the cops, *something*, just do something different!" But they didn't. Travis had a way of manipulating my mom into giving him whatever he wanted, and she hid everything from my dad. I always felt stuck in the middle and frustrated that they just wouldn't listen to me.

His addiction was so bad that there were times I would say to God, "If he's going to die, just take him because we can no longer live this way." My dad was always angry. My mom was always sad. Her sole mission in life was to keep him alive just one more day. It was like our souls — our identities — were ripped out of us, and our purpose in life was to go through the motions and hope nothing tragic happened.

There were even times we were fearful that, if the drugs didn't kill him, he'd kill himself. Mom would wake up in the morning and find letters like this addressed to her on the kitchen table:

Mom,

I can't control it, Mom. I knew it was wrong. I knew it would fuck me over. I knew you would hate me, despise me, and want me out of the house. I knew all this, but I could not stop myself from doing it. Mom, I'm completely fucked up in the head. Something is seriously wrong with me.

I'm actually crying while I'm writing this. Mom, I need your help. I am working for cash tomorrow, maybe Friday, and definitely Saturday and Sunday. If I do not have $250 dollars in your hand by Sunday night, you can tell Dad or do whatever you feel is right. I keep digging myself in a deeper hole, and I can't get out. Yesterday I could not control myself and that scares the living shit out of me. I am going to end up like Steve [a close friend of Travis's who died of an overdose] or worse. I am not going to live to be an old man the way I'm going. I did not rob [the Smiths], but I am guilty of being a horrible, lying sack of shit that does not deserve a pot to piss in.

Mom, I'm scared, and I don't know what to do. If I lose this house and/or this job, I'll kill myself. I will be absolutely lost, Mom. I won't go out anymore. I'll have my cell phone shut off. I won't even see Kira. No matter what, I will have the money in your hand by Sunday. I have to leave Saturday so I can finish the job and get paid. Then I'll stay home. I'll do whatever you need no matter how shitty or small the job is, and I'll do it when you ask.

As soon as I get back onto Suboxone, things will change drastically. I will force myself to take it so even if I wanted to do pills, it wouldn't even matter.

I am ruining my life Mom, and I'm making you hate me so much that you might never feel the same way about me again, no matter how well I do.

I know it doesn't mean anything. None of this does. All I'm asking for is three days. Just give me three days to get the money back to you. If I don't, you can turn me into the police if you want to.

Mom, I will seriously kill myself if you turn your back on me. I hate what I am doing, and I hate what I am becoming. If you disown me, then I have nothing left. And what will push me over the edge is knowing I could have stopped it. I did it all. I killed myself.

To get letters from your child saying, "If you don't do this, I'm going to kill myself," must be one of the hardest things to try to deal with. I very much sympathized with her, but I was also pissed at Travis for manipulating her like that.

Once again, even as an adult, I felt stuck between supporting my parents as they struggled with my brother's addiction, my own struggles with his addiction, and trying to grow up and lead my own life.

Six months after moving back home, I was twenty-one years old, had no friends, and spent my time working and going to a community college. I had no life because I'd given up everything I loved for my ex-boyfriend. My mom worked at a bank, and I would frequently stop in to visit her. One day her co-worker, someone I knew from stopping in so often, invited me to come to a local bar and see her friend's band play. My mom had shared with her how I had recently ended a five-year relationship and had no friends.

I decided to go see the band, and that night changed my life forever. I was afraid to go alone, so I invited one of my co-workers to join me. At the last minute, something came up and she backed out. Because I had already committed to going, I went by myself. When I pulled up, I sat in my car for thirty minutes before getting out. But I did it, I mustered up the courage and walked into that bar. The band was amazing; I had so much fun and met a guy, Ryan, the lead singer of the band. He invited me to go to his show the following night, which I happily agreed to attend.

I remember the second night vividly. Ryan was asking me about my family when I blurted out, "My brother is addicted to drugs." I think that was the first time I verbalized that to someone other than my family. I don't know why I felt the need to share that information with him, but I did. Thankfully, he was unfazed. We started dating shortly after.

Luckily for me, I had learned from my past mistakes and decided to take this relationship slow and *not* give up who I was for a guy. After dating for a year, we moved in together. One year later, we bought a house together. Ten months after that, we got married.

My wedding was another challenging time. It's hard to plan such an important part of your life when someone in your immediate family is struggling. I felt like my parents were only half in.

At my bachelorette party, we had just finished getting massages and were on our way to dinner when my mom received a phone call from one of Travis's friends. Travis was in jail. Again. Even though there was nothing my mom could do, I knew at that moment I had lost her. She was no longer truly present, just going through the motions. For me, it was just another moment that was stolen from me due to my brother's actions.

For my wedding, Ryan and I made the decision that Travis would not be a groomsman — probably one of the toughest decisions in my life. Travis was currently at his worst, to the point we didn't think he would even live. We were afraid that, if we had him in the wedding and he died before the wedding, we would have to explain why we had a missing groomsman. He did end up attending the wedding, but, unfortunately, he was as high as a kite.

A month after my wedding, and after many years of riding the addiction rollercoaster, my parents finally mustered up the courage to kick him out of the house. It was another really scary time in our journey because, after that, we didn't know where he was or what he was doing, or even if he was alive. Then again, we just spent the last five years or more thinking the same exact thing. The only difference now was that he couldn't come home.

We don't know what happened during that time period, but, from the stories he told us, he started living in a drug house. About two weeks after my parents kicked him out, my mom gave him a call and gave him two options: option one — keep doing what you are doing and you're no longer a part of this family; option two — get help. That day, he decided to enter treatment.

When he decided to go into treatment, it was a huge relief, yet, at the same time, I doubted very much that he was going to follow through. He'd already been through so many counselors and previous treatment programs, why would this one work?

Treatment was tough, not only for him but for us as a family. He spent two weeks in detox because they couldn't get his heart rate to stabilize. He also made numerous calls to my mom that he wanted to leave because he hated it there and came up with many reasons why he should leave. But she stuck to her guns and did not rescue him. I, for the first time ever, felt that things were really going to change.

We had to go to family sessions, which I feel are absolutely necessary. We made tremendous progress during those meetings. Travis spent ninety days in detox and residential treatment, then moved to a sober-living home. He never went back to my parents' house.

So much happened between high school and the "end" when my parents kicked Travis out. He had seen numerous counselors, been in and out of jail, gone missing, and so on. I cannot remember it all. It's probably repressed somewhere in my brain, but chances are you've heard the same story told by many people.

Recovery

The beginning part of Travis's recovery was fairly rough. We all assumed that he would go into treatment and come out healthy and be the person he was before he started using drugs. No one can really prepare you for the changes an addict has to go through, nor the changes you have to make.

Travis came out of treatment drug and alcohol free, but he still had that arrogant, manipulative personality he had while he was using substances. Because of this, three months after completing treatment, he started drinking again thinking he could "handle it," but he couldn't, and he received his third DUI. Yet even after getting caught drinking, he still wanted to cheat the system. He entered the alcohol treatment court, submitted all the required breathalyzers, but forged signatures for all of the required meetings he was supposed to attend. Looking back at this now, I feel as though I should have said something to him, encouraged him to go to the meetings.

But as time went on, his personality started to change. He became humble and loved being sober. It was like he had a new passion for life.

After he left treatment, he lived in a sober-living home for a while, then eventually got his own apartment with a girl, Cindy, he started dating when he got out of treatment.

Because he received his third DUI, he lost his driver's license which meant that we had to drive him to all of his appointments and court dates. I don't think anyone minded because we were just happy to have him back. Besides, I think not having a car to go out and buy drugs helped him maintain his sobriety. Sure, he could have had the drugs delivered, but I think the lack of freedom really helped him stay sober.

My husband and I went on our honeymoon to Mexico around the time that Travis got out of inpatient treatment. On one of the last days of our trip, my mom called me with this "brilliant idea" that she had. That ten-minute phone call cost me $40.

Her idea was to start sharing our story, or at least to have Travis share his story, with young kids. Because we'd had very little education on substances and the consequences, she thought by sharing the *true* consequences — not the stuff you see in movies — we could prevent other kids from living the nightmare that we lived through. Travis was on board, and so was I. But there was no way in hell I would ever set foot on a stage.

Two months after I got back from my honeymoon, I found out I was pregnant. I was incredibly excited! I also graduated from college that month with a Bachelor of Human Resources. My dream was to work in human resources or be a corporate trainer, although that never came to fruition.

A few weeks after finding out that I was pregnant, Travis and Cindy found out that they were expecting, too. While it was super exciting news, it was also kind of scary. Travis was only a couple months into recovery, and we didn't know if he would be able to maintain his sobriety.

That summer, we started working on mom's idea of sharing stories. We talked with some school administrators, invited some kids over for trials, and found others in recovery that were also interested in sharing their stories. We honestly had no idea what we were doing, but that didn't stop us. We were passionate, and I think people felt that.

As we worked on this project, my relationship with Travis started to strengthen. While I didn't fully trust him yet, I did see that he wanted to turn his story into something positive. He really wanted to help prevent kids from going down the path that he did.

That fall, my parents bought a house one house down from mine that Travis and Cindy rented from them. Being geographically close to Travis further strengthened our relationship. It was easy to just walk over to his house and hang out. I also liked the fact that I could keep a close eye on him and check on him whenever I wanted.

Cindy and I spent our pregnancies going to swimming classes, yoga, and getting ready to welcome our boys into this world.

My family also decided to bring our program, which we named Your Choice to Live Inc., into a few local middle schools. We obviously had some learning and tweaking to do, but overall, it was very well received.

I remember one particular presentation at a local middle school. During the question-and-answer section, a seventh grade girl asked Travis how his sister felt during all of this. I had *never* been asked this question, and I was totally unprepared. I had refused to speak publicly because public speaking is scary to me. But I walked in front of the crowd and, while I don't remember what I said exactly, let it out. I was crying (it could have been the pregnancy hormones), but I shared that I'd felt neglected and angry. I think it was a shock to my parents because not once had I ever vocalized my feelings before. I never went to a counselor to deal with what I was feeling during my brother's use. Looking back, I probably should have.

I gave birth to my son, Nolan, in January, 2010, and Cindy had their son, Kasen, in February. Since we lived close by, we spent a lot of time together.

Sometime before the boys' second birthdays, Travis and Cindy broke up. I watched my nephew a few days a week and saw Cindy when she came to pick him up, but we did not maintain our relationship. I'll be honest here, my loyalty was to my brother. Travis and Cindy went to mediation and agreed on a custody placement schedule.

On April 22, 2011, my second child, Teagan, was born. That same day, Travis got his license back. It was an exciting time but also a scary time because we didn't know what he would do with this freedom. He had more access to substances than before — would he go back to using? But he didn't. He'd had the time he needed to make changes in his life for the better.

A few years later, Travis filed for a custody placement change, requesting that Kasen have more time with him. While I supported his decision to have more time with his son, I did not play a part in the custody case. The court found no reason to change placement, so it stayed fifty-fifty custody. I thought, *If Travis can get through this without using substances, he can get through anything*. I also made it blatantly clear to him that if he ever started using again, I would tell Cindy because my loyalty was first to his son.

While Travis and Cindy's relationship was never great, they went to counseling together and seemed to find common ground.

Your Choice to Live Inc. grew and officially became a non-profit in 2012. For the past three years, we had only been sharing stories of recovery. Then I started speaking about being a sibling. We eventually included my parents sharing their story so that kids could see how one person's choice could ripple through a family. We met some really great people who helped us along the way. We went from sharing our family story with kids, to developing programs for parents, teachers, professionals, and community members.

One of our most powerful programs, "Stairway to Heroin," included the four of us sitting on stools together sharing our stories from each of our sides — the substance user, the sister, the mom, and the dad. For the twenty-five minutes that we shared the darkest parts of our lives and the hope that we had once Travis found recovery, you could hear a pin drop and see the tears rolling down people's faces. After the presentation, many parents would come up and thank us for giving them hope. Others would say that they wished they were as lucky as us, that they had lost their loved one.

Our stories made a difference. They had a huge impact on students, parents, teachers, and community members. By

2016, we were averaging over two hundred presentations a year, reaching over 50,000 annually throughout the Midwest.

As Your Choice to Live Inc. grew, so did my relationship with my brother. We spent almost every day speaking in schools. We spent all our free time hanging out with our kids. Our family unit also became stronger. When Travis wasn't speaking with me, he was helping our dad with the family landscaping business. Sure, we had our normal family issues, but we were stronger than ever.

And Travis loved helping others find sobriety. After presentations, struggling students would reach out to Travis for advice. Parents would email us asking for next steps. Travis would help guide that child/teen/adult to see that recovery is possible and life is better sober.

My parents and I were so proud of him for overcoming his addiction and moving forward with his life.

I ended up moving out of the subdivision in 2014, four days before I gave birth to my third child, Tenley. Although I was only fifteen minutes away from Travis, I missed being right next door to him. I was grateful that we worked together because we still got to see each other almost every single day.

Two years later, our entire family traveled to Sedona, Arizona, for Travis's wedding. Travis and his fiancé, Karen, had gone to high school together. Karen was a no-bullshit type girl that never used drugs. She pushed him to go to college, wanting him to continuously work on being a better person. We were excited that he had found someone like her. I was honored when Travis asked me to be the best "man" in his wedding.

A few years later, Travis and Karen welcomed their baby girl, Maggie, *on my birthday*! It was the best birthday gift ever. When Maggie got sick as a newborn, I spent the day with her in the hospital while Karen and Travis got some rest. When they went on vacation, I would take care of her. I even watched her one day a week during the summer so that I could build a bond with her.

As Travis started to build his family and we moved away from each other, we began spending less time together, which, to me, was totally normal. Most people don't spend all of their time with family members. We each had our own families. I didn't notice any red flags.

For the first time in years, I finally felt that I had my family back, and I did everything I could to protect that.

Relapse

The weekend before we found out about Travis's relapse, Mom had babysat that Saturday night while Travis and Karen went out to dinner. She had a gut feeling something was off with Travis. When they returned from dinner, Travis immediately went and laid on the couch. This was not a typical thing for him to do. Usually, he's a bundle of energy, always engaging in some sort of conversation. This was a red flag. Because of her suspicions, Mom asked Karen to step out to the garage and point-blank asked her if Travis had been drinking or using drugs. Karen looked her dead in the eye and said, "Absolutely not."

Mom called me on her way home that night pretty upset because she knew something was up. Since Travis and I had a pretty good relationship, I texted him asking if everything was okay. He called me back about thirty minutes later and told me that he was acting strange because Karen had a miscarriage. Ok, that made sense. This was a legit reason to seem off. I did not want to believe my mom's gut instinct that something was wrong.

Travis and I ended up going out for coffee the next morning, something we did regularly when he was struggling with something going on. He proceeded to tell me that, besides the miscarriage, Karen also caught him exchanging inappropriate pictures with her brother's girlfriend. Truthfully, I wasn't surprised. He always spent a lot of time on his phone, and when I'd caught glimpses of his phone, I'd seen some of the pictures he'd exchanged with other women and the conversations he'd had with them. So, for me, this was nothing new, but, for some reason, he seemed to be pretty down about this one. It could have been because he was finally caught, yet I couldn't put my finger on it. I even asked him if he was using drugs, and he said, "Absolutely not." He kept saying, "You don't really know me. I have a darker side." And I was thinking, *Really bro*? *I'm pretty sure I know about your past and what you do on the side. I do know you, probably more than anyone else in this entire world.* Little did I know that, four days later, I would learn the hard reality that I didn't know my brother at all.

August 22, 2019, was a day I will never forget, although I wish I could. That day started off amazing. A good friend of ours brought in a national speaker, Luke, to speak to the LaCrosse area businesses, community members, and school districts about the impact of marijuana legalization. I was asked to open the presentation with information on vaping. This was a huge honor for me. I got to "open" for a national speaker! The presentation was being held three hours away, so my mom, Melanie (our good friend and co-worker), and I left in the morning. I presented my part during the day presentation with Luke to follow. We then had the opportunity to go out to lunch with Luke before the evening presentation. After the last presentation, we headed home. Mom was driving. About twenty minutes into the drive, Melanie questioned Mom about where we were going since none of the scenery seemed familiar. So we double checked the GPS, and sure enough, we were headed to 440 S. Lapham, *Iowa*, not Wisconsin! We laughed so hard because this was a typical Sandi thing, then turned around.

About an hour into our trip home, Mom received a panicked phone call from Travis's wife. Karen stated that Travis had been drinking, and she was worried that he was going to hurt himself, her, or his two children. We were in absolute shock! I don't even know what we initially said. I do know that we pulled over right away and Melanie took over the driving.

Karen proceeded to tell us that Travis had started drinking occasionally on their honeymoon three years earlier. In the beginning, he could drink occasionally, but then he started to do it more often. Then it got to the point where they would have a few drinks together, go to bed, and once she would fall asleep, he would get back up to drink until he passed out. Karen said she felt bad because she had been encouraging him to drink.

On this particular night, Travis had gone to pick up Chinese. food for dinner When he returned home fifteen minutes later, he pulled into the driveway and smashed into her car. She didn't understand how he could get so drunk in such a short amount of time. Even after she confronted him, he continued to drink. The point at which she decided to call my mom was when he was threatening to kill himself.

Our immediate reaction was to advise her to call 911. She had two children in the house that she needed to protect. But she did not.

He took off with his friends, and she had no idea where he went.

We finally made it back to town around 11:30 p.m. exhausted, but, at the same time, our adrenaline was running high. We dropped Melanie off and decided to go to Travis and Karen's house. I mean, what else were we supposed to do? We just got the most devastating news that Travis was using again and was missing. We drove around looking for him and were about to head home when we saw a car drop him off.

The memory of seeing him drunk will forever bring tears to my eyes. He stumbled out of the car missing a shoe and yelling at Karen for telling us his secret. We tried to talk to him and let him know that we loved him and would help him find help, but he wasn't having it. He stumbled into his house and went to bed.

Before we got to Travis's house, Mom and I had decided that we were not going to tell Dad that night. He was probably sleeping, and we would discuss what happened in the morning. We didn't know that Karen had called the house phone (that no one ever calls) which woke him up. He called us, so we briefly told him what was going on, although we did downplay it. When we were leaving Travis's subdivision after our encounter with him, Dad drove by, but we told him to go home since his presence wouldn't help the situation at all.

With all the emotions from the past happening again — Dad angry because he was scared, Mom being upset — I cried all the way home. I'd had the longest day ever, but I could not go to sleep. Every time I laid in my bed and closed my eyes, the tears would pour down my cheeks. To take my mind off of it, I got up and watched TV. I believe I fell asleep around 4 a.m.

Words cannot describe the betrayal I felt. I've never been cheated on in my life, but I can imagine it feels the same. Here was someone I loved more than anything in the world, someone I've defended for the past ten years and taken time away from my family to help, and, in one phone call, my world came crashing down. I could not fathom how he could lie to me for the past three years and be okay with that. I was also super pissed because, for the past two years, he had been sharing his story with students and families pretending that he was sober, when he wasn't.

The next day, I felt like I woke up from the worst nightmare I had ever had, except it was real life. I immediately texted my best friend and co-worker, Katie, who is also in recovery.

"I have some very bad news to tell you. We just found out last night that Travis relapsed. Supposedly he's been drinking "socially" since his honeymoon, but he can't control it anymore. I'm so pissed, hurt, and sad right now."

But I couldn't dwell on it. I had to pull myself together and pretend like nothing happened because I had three precious children that needed me that day. So I did exactly that. I'm sure they sensed something was up, but they didn't say anything. When my husband came home after work, I locked myself in the bathroom and cried for an hour. The pain was unreal.

I wasn't really angry about the drinking. I have always said from day one of his recovery that, at any moment, he could go back to using. Relapse is common, and I understand that. What hurt me so badly was that he hid it from me and lied to me about it. From that point on, I felt like our whole relationship was a lie and questioned everything he ever did or said. I even questioned if he was ever even sober. I don't think I'll ever know that answer.

As hard as it was for me, I cannot imagine what my parents were going through. Mom woke up and ran to Travis's house the next day. She wanted to figure out how to help him. He was pretty adamant that it was a one-time thing and that he didn't need help. The miscarriage really had him down, and he chose the wrong way to cope. Since he'd already lost one baby, having another miscarriage probably triggered trauma from years ago. He didn't seek help.

The next few weeks were up and down. I got a call from him one day, and he was pretty upset. I vividly remember sitting at the end of my driveway listening to him. I always tried to keep my kids away from my brother's struggles with addiction because they were too young, and, because they loved their uncle so much, I didn't want them to see him struggle. So there I was, sitting at the end of my driveway which is super long and at the end of a dead-end road. He kept telling me that he was upset about the miscarriage, and he didn't know if he could stay married to Karen. He proceeded to tell me that he expected me to call him every morning to check in with him. Then he started blaming me and our parents for his drinking! I was shocked. I had *no* idea where this was coming from. He then claimed he had just met with his therapist who told him he needed to have a six-pack of beer as a last hurrah. At that moment, it all made sense. He had been drinking.

After that, things seemed to go okay. We were still in communication, he was seeing a new therapist, and things were starting to look up (at least from what we could tell).

I know that my mom, especially, got her hopes up. She desperately wanted to believe Travis when he said he was sober and doing well. But I didn't trust him. I became very frustrated with the situation because I was again trying to be the voice of reason, and again it was mostly falling on deaf ears. I was angry that Mom could just jump right in and trust him so quickly, knowing that he'd lied to her for three years. I mean, I wanted him to be doing well, don't get me wrong, but deep inside I knew it was likely manipulation. I wanted to believe his words, but his actions didn't line up.

During this time period, I "lost" my mother. I couldn't go to her with my hurt because, even though she understood the pain I was going through, she was also suffering. The last thing I wanted to do was cause her more pain. It felt like we went right back to where we were when Travis was a teenager. I was back in the shadows, and she was back to trying to get him sober. Keeping him sober became her number one priority.

As for my dad, he was angry because he saw the pain my mother was going through *again*. He was quiet about the situation and shut down. My brother continued to work for him, but they never talked about what happened. Travis wanted to sweep it under the rug like nothing ever happened, and my dad didn't want to go back ten years and relive everything. I would say their relationship changed to an employer/employee relationship because the father/son relationship was, once again, lost.

On October 17, 2019, I was in an executive board meeting when I got a call from my dad. My dad rarely calls me, so I excused myself and took the call. Dad thought Travis had been drinking. He didn't have proof, but they were at work, and he could smell alcohol in the cab of the skid-steer. After the board meeting, I shared the news with my mom. Her instinct was to go confront him, but this time she took with her an alcohol swab, which tests for presence of alcohol by swabbing the saliva in the mouth. She expected him to lie, and she wanted proof. Low and behold, it was positive for alcohol, and my dad later found a bottle of Fireball cinnamon whiskey in the dump truck. (Yes, Travis drove the dump truck to work.) No one but Travis knew when he'd started drinking that day, but that was the last time he was ever allowed to work for my father. Despite having a positive test, Travis denied drinking up and down and left the job with a friend.

Karen was at work that day, but Mom called and left her a message letting her know what happened. Mom and I had a presentation that night down in Illinois. I *swear* every time we had a presentation, something happened. On our travels, we received a call from Karen. She told us she had talked to Travis and believed he did not drink and drive so there was no issue for her. She then proceeded to tell us that the only reason he drinks is because he can't stand us — his family. She said, and I quote, "Alcohol is not the problem — you guys are."

At that point, I had a major "ah-ha" moment. For the past four years, he had been telling us that he cannot stand his wife, that she is awful to him. All the while, he was telling *her* that he cannot stand *us*, and *we* are awful to him. By essentially keeping us apart, he could continue doing the things he wanted to do, and we were none the wiser. And, to be honest, this master plan worked for three years.

I was really frustrated with the phone call. Karen knew nothing about addiction, and here she was blaming us. WTF? At the end of the conversation, I said if we truly were the problem, not the alcohol, then we would remove ourselves from their lives, and that should solve all their problems.

Travis tried calling us after our conversation with her, but we ignored the call. Sounds cold, but we were just so shocked since this was the first time we'd *ever* heard this. We also didn't want to return to previous habits and jump in to try to save him. We had a good friend at the time, who's a counselor and also in long-term recovery, tell us not to rescue him — he needs to find his way himself.

So that's what we did. Was it easy? *Hell* no. We love him so much that we want to help. But we realized that there was nothing more we could do. For the past three months, we had loved him, provided guidance, and listened to him with his struggles. That obviously wasn't helping because he was still drinking and blaming us for all the wrong in his life. It was time to change things up.

Making the decision to let him go was difficult, but I still had one more difficult decision to make. I had to decide if I wanted to tell the mother of his first-born child that he was drinking. I knew that Travis's drinking was more out of hand than anyone wanted to admit. He'd been operating heavy equipment under the influence, and I couldn't fathom what else he was capable of doing.

My nephew means the world to me, and I was afraid for his safety. Most people reading this would probably say, *It's a no-brainer; you have to tell her*, but I really struggled with the decision.

Before I get into the decision I made, I'd like to take a step back and explain the relationship between Travis and the mother of his first-born, Cindy. I think it's good to have some context to understand the situation.

Travis and Cindy had a pretty rocky relationship after they split up. After a nasty court battle and some time to heal, their relationship started to mend. As time went on, he would stop by her house to check on her, send her snap chats, or sit with her at football practices. I hadn't seen or talked to Cindy after they split up until our boys started playing football together in August 2019. Every practice, Cindy and I would at least make an effort to say hi to each other and catch up. We were slowly starting to build up a relationship, even if it was just surface level. I think Kasen even found it pretty cool that his mom, dad, aunt, uncle, cousins, and grandparents could all be in one place and get along. Everything was going great among all parties.

Since everything was going so well, I didn't want to mess anything up. But keeping his drinking a secret was making me sick. I thought through every single angle. Should I call Travis and tell him that if he doesn't tell, I will? But then I thought, will he be truthful? Then I thought about what would happen if I didn't tell her — would he drink before he picked up Kasen? I asked my counselor friend his opinion, and my parents, my in-laws, and my friends. I even made a chart of pros and cons.

My biggest concern was the safety of my nephew, and I didn't believe that Travis would tell Cindy the truth because then he could lose his son. If Cindy got full custody of Kasen, there was a huge chance I would never see him again. However, I would rather lose the opportunity to see my nephew than to have something horrible happen to him because I never said anything.

On October 20, three days after the dump truck incident, I made the decision to tell Cindy. I still had her number, although

I didn't know if she had changed it. I made the call that Sunday, but she didn't answer, and I didn't leave a message. I didn't want to give her a heads up and risk her calling Travis so he could spin it his own way. The next day I called again, and this time I left a message just asking her to call me back. She immediately called me back, and I invited her to my house.

Let me tell you, that was the one of the longest days of my life. By the time she got to my house, I was shaking. We sat out on my deck, and I told her everything I knew. I was expecting her to be super pissed and ready to take him back to court. But that is not what happened. She was super sad. We all loved the sober, healthy Travis. And she knew how important Travis was to Kasen. We invited my mom to join us at my house then came up with a plan.

That plan was to do an intervention. Cindy was to invite Travis out for coffee (nothing new for them), and Mom and I would show up. Needless to say, it was another long day, and I felt like I was going to puke. I can't even imagine what my mom was going through. The plan was going accordingly. They met for coffee, we walked into the coffee shop, and he immediately got up and walked out.

I know what some of you are thinking, *Did you really think that was going to work?* For those of you that have never been in this situation, you are willing to try anything to get someone you love help.

Anyway, we followed him outside. He asked us how we could do this to him. We, of course, told him we loved him and wanted him to get help. He looked right at Mom and said, "You have lost your son." I felt bad for my mom at that moment because I was the one that told Cindy. It was my fault, not my mom's. She didn't make that decision, I did, but my mom was the one that got the wrath. Then he walked to his truck and left.

After that meeting, I had another "ah-ha" moment. Not only was he keeping Karen and us separated, but he was keeping Cindy from communicating with us as well. We weren't talking to Karen because of the things he told us about her, and Karen wasn't talking to us because of the things he told her about us. And the way to keep Cindy quiet was to be super nice to her so Cindy wouldn't ask any questions because everything seemed great.

That day, when two of his three worlds came together, he knew his ruse was over. Our biggest mistake was not including Karen. Even though Karen strongly believed he didn't have a problem with alcohol, having her there would have made all his worlds collide. Though it's possible nothing would have changed.

Cindy and Travis met up a few days later, and he promised to get help if she kept it out of court, and she agreed. He also asked her not to have a relationship with us, his family. Cindy agreed because she wanted him to get help, but she didn't keep her promise. She didn't feel that it was in Kasen's best interest to be kept away from his aunt, cousins, and grandparents who were all very important in his life. Cindy even met with Karen who, at that time, promised to let Cindy know if Travis started drinking again. Things from that point on seemed to go as planned.

I didn't have much communication from Travis after this. He was so angry that I told Cindy (and still is). That is something I will have to live with for the rest of my life. Yet I don't, for one second, regret that decision. I feel to my core it was absolutely the right decision. At the end of the day, I never would have had to make this decision if he hadn't been drinking. The only communication I had with him then was to ask if Kasen could come play with his cousins, which he did allow.

That fall, my parents decided to head to Florida for Thanksgiving. We traditionally don't celebrate Thanksgiving day together because I'm usually with my in-laws, but we do get together as a family on the Friday after. But my parents were upfront and honest that they were running from the memories of past holidays. If they went somewhere else, it was like the holiday never happened. They wouldn't sit at home expecting a "Happy Thanksgiving" call or text. We'd had enough awful holidays back in the day, and they didn't want any more holidays like that. They knew that Christmas was right around the corner, and this would be the first Christmas that Travis wouldn't be around, which we viewed as a bittersweet situation. We didn't want the drama, but it would also be the first Christmas in 33 years he wouldn't be there.

When they told me their plans to head south, I'm not going to lie, my heart sank a little bit. I felt deserted. Like, *Hey, I'm hurting too, but I have children that like to spend their holidays with their grandparents. Why do they also have to suffer because of his choice?* I also panicked a little bit thinking that they would run for Christmas as well, or that they would be sad and my children would feel the weight of that.

As we approached Christmas, my parents promised they wouldn't leave. Instead of dreading the upcoming holiday, we decided that it was time to switch things up and start new traditions. So we did exactly that. It turned out to be the most fun and most relaxed Christmas we'd had in a long time. I guess I didn't realize how much Travis's and Karen's moods affected us all in prior years. I sent Christmas gifts to their daughter, and my kids made them cards. Yet my kids never even got a call or were even acknowledged by their uncle.

In January 2020, we went to Disney for my son's tenth birthday. It was absolutely amazing. We had so much fun, and it was such a nice break from reality and the craziness of our lives. Little did we know that, two months later, the world would shut down due to COVID-19.[1]

On my son's birthday, while we were at Hollywood Studios, I got a call from my brother. I didn't answer because I hadn't heard from him in months. I later received a text that he wanted to wish my son a happy birthday. I didn't reply. I wasn't going to allow him to be in and out of my children's lives. At this point, it was better that he was out. A month later, during a family

---

1 The SARS-CoV-2 virus, commonly known as COVID or COVID-19, started a pandemic at the beginning of 2020 and was still active up through the publication of this book. The measures taken to thwart the virus were considered extreme at times and disrupted life and the living patterns of all who experienced it.

meeting, I got an earful about how awful I was because I didn't let them say happy birthday to my son on his birthday.

After the Disney trip and the months of no communication with Travis, I started to feel confused. I had not spoken to Travis since October, and I was starting to question whether or not he knew the *real* reason why no one from our family was talking to him. Had Karen told him about our conversation with her on October 17 when she told us that we were the problem, not the alcohol?

I also didn't want any confrontation with him. I just wanted him to hear from me why we decided to walk away. So I decided to write him a letter and send it in the mail. Here is what I wrote:

> Mom, Dad, and I have been there for you through every up and every down. I have dropped everything to help you move, spend time at the hospital with your daughter when she was sick, watch the kids, or meet you for coffee/lunch because you were depressed. Mom and Dad have not only supported you financially, but have always supported your choices.
>
> On October 17, when you were caught drinking at work, Mom called Karen. Karen called back while Mom and I were together. Karen told both of us how much you truly hated us. The alcohol was not the problem — we were. We tried to explain to her that those were just excuses so that you could drink. But she was ADAMANT that you hated us and always have. I understand that Karen doesn't understand addiction, but imagine how that made us feel. My personal opinion is that you told her you drink because of us, and you told us you drink because you can't stand her, just so that you could keep us apart.
>
> So we made the decision as a family that, if you really hated us and we were the true reason you drank, then we would remove ourselves from your life. Then that should solve all the problems. We'd rather you be sober and healthy than in our lives and drinking.

We all miss the old Travis — the Travis from a couple years ago. In hindsight, we should have known something was up. I just thought you were getting cockier and more arrogant and that was the person you were going to be. But really, you were cocky and arrogant because you were getting away with your drinking. Hopefully one day, when you truly get sober, that old Travis will come back.

I know you told Mom and Dad to "get over it" and "move on," but saying that totally dismisses all the hurt you've caused all of us. It's selfish, and, in order for everyone to move on, you have to admit and address what you did wrong. Deep down inside you know that's such a cowardly thing to do. You have to man up and admit that you were wrong.

And just for the record — I will NEVER apologize for telling Cindy. I have always told you, if you ever went back to drinking or using drugs, I would tell her. Kasen means more to me than you or her, and I had to do what is best for Kasen. Cindy's actually been really mature about this and putting Kasen first. You should be thankful for that. The only person who gets hurt in this situation is Kasen. We are all adults and can move on with our lives, but Kasen doesn't understand, and he is suffering. I wish you would agree to counseling for him so that he has an outlet, someone outside of the family to talk to. By not agreeing to it, it only proves that you have something to hide. He needs his dad, and you're not there for him. From his eyes, work is more important to you than he is.

I don't want anything from this letter — a call, text, or letter. I wrote this more for me to get things off my chest and let you go. My hope is one day you grow a set of balls, drop your pride, and own up to what you did and the pain you caused. I don't want anything to do with you until you sober up and the old — like three years ago old — Travis comes back. Otherwise, have a nice life.

Typing and sending that letter was a huge weight off my chest. For the first time, I felt like I got to tell him how I felt. I also felt that, if something were to happen to him, I could live with myself because I would have peace knowing he knew how I felt.

A month after our Disney trip, it was Kasen's tenth birthday. Since we didn't hear anything from Travis in regard to birthday plans, we made our own plans to celebrate his birthday with Cindy. Kasen had a blast spending time with us.

Well, when Travis and Karen heard from Kasen that he spent his birthday with us, all hell broke loose. Karen sent my mother an awful text, so we said, "Let's have a family meeting." So we did.

At this time, I hadn't seen Travis or Karen in probably five months, and they came in guns blazing. Before I go any farther, let me tell you, this was a bad idea. If you ever plan on doing a family meeting like this, have professionals with you!

Anyway, we wanted to hear their side, and we wanted them to know ours. The meeting started off with the whole how-could-I-tell-Cindy complaint. I explained that it was the right thing to do.

At some point during the meeting, Travis got mad and left. And I, as embarrassed as I am to admit it, yelled, "Don't be a coward, and come back and talk to us!" I was furious that he just couldn't listen to our side. All he and Karen did was blame us. He took absolutely no responsibility and denied ever drinking. I even broke down and cried and told him how much I missed him — the healthy, happy person he once was — and he laughed in my face.

That meeting was another heartbreak for us. Prior to the meeting, we thought, *Ok, this is going to be it. He'll hear our side, we'll hear his side, and we can find some common ground.* That obviously didn't happen.

By now, we were so lost, confused, and hurt. Just like most people who are in this situation, we wanted to find a reason — an answer for all of this. We had shared our experience with the relapse with some of our counselor friends, and they told us that, maybe, he may also have a mental health disorder causing him to not see the wrong in his actions. So what did we do? We bought every book on common personality disorders — narcissism, antisocial personality disorder, borderline personality disorder, and so on. By the end of our "research," we had him diagnosed as a narcissistic psychopath with borderline personality disorder.

Let me give you some examples. In the book, *I Hate You — Don't Leave Me: Understanding the Borderline Personality* by Jerold J. Kreisman and Hal Straus, it says that people with borderline personality disorder don't like to take responsibility, so they create a "damned if I do, damned if I don't" situation, which is exactly what Travis would do.

In *Psychopath Free: Recovering from Emotionally Abusive Relationships With Narcissists, Sociopaths, and Other Toxic People*, author Jackson MacKenzie says that a psychopath will keep each target far enough apart so that they can't compare notes, but close enough that they're always on edge and unsure where they stand. This is exactly what Travis did with Mom, me, Cindy, and Karen.

I think, when something isn't right, people tend to look for a diagnosis or label to "explain" why someone acts the way they do. That was us. Really, though, it didn't help at all. He could have any one of those disorders, but it doesn't make me feel any better.

Twenty-seven days after our disastrous family meeting, I got a text from Travis: "Let's meet." It was a Sunday night, I was spending time with my family, and, with the way things went the last time we met, I really didn't want to give up any more of my family time to meet with him. I'd done it too many times in the past, and I didn't want to do it again. I texted him, "I don't have time to meet with you, but I can call you after the kids go to bed, and we can talk on the phone."

No response.

A few hours later, I received an email from him:

Ashleigh,

I'm writing you this letter because I want to know what else you're looking for from me. I sincerely apologized for my actions over the last few years [he did not]. I have made an attempt to talk this out with you in person, and you didn't want to. I have reached out to see your kids — what else do you need me to do?

In your letter to me, you stated that you wanted the old Travis back or it's "have a nice life." The old Travis is not coming back because I am a different person now. I'm still your brother, but I am not the same person that I used to be. Since everything has happened, I, for the first time in my life, do not need my family's approval or assistance. It is freeing and liberating. I'm not sure if anyone in the family truly grasps how hard it was to be constantly pulled in opposite directions by the same people.

I have been seeking continuous help in the areas of my life that have been hurting me inside. What seemed like simple decisions to you and Mom were monumental decisions to me. I may have talked it to death, but I needed to, and neither you nor Mom were there to help. Instead, all I heard was, "I don't want to hear about it anymore." So I didn't talk, and I kept it inside, and it killed me. Things happen for a reason, and, thankfully, I will never have to make that choice again.

I have been on medication for mental illness for a couple of months now, and it has been a life changer. I am able to relax, focus, and stay level-headed without the fear of certain doom. The anxiety that was affecting me has been put in check, leaving me with a clear view of my goals and my future.

Along with medication, I have been seeing a therapist to help cope with any of the other issues I am having trouble dealing with.

I have started my business back up, and it is going incredibly well. I feel a sense of purpose in the work that I do, and I am really enjoying it. It has been keeping me busy and motivated. I have never been in a better place than I am right now.

The reason I say I will never be the same person I used to be is because I am stronger now than I have ever been in all aspects of my life. I have been completely sober and mentally sound for months now. I do not drink at all and drugs never come into the picture.

It is up to you whether you want to believe me or not. Just know that I do not *need* you to believe me — I believe in myself. Would I like you to believe me? Absolutely, but the ball is in your court.

Finally, I asked you nicely not to have a relationship with Cindy. I have not asked you for anything besides this. The reason I don't want you to have a relationship with her is because it creates drama between Cindy and me, which in turn affects Kasen. For example, you reached out to Cindy last night and told her Karter was sleeping over and called her so they could talk. Why would you reach out? All that did was cause me to get a phone call at 10 p.m. asking, "Why did you tell Karen we aren't going to Disney? I wanted to tell him." If Kasen ever wants to talk to his mom, or she wants to talk to him, they are more than welcome to do so with me, and they both know this. If you have questions for her about my mental stability, or she has questions for you, feel free to chat away. You are not Kasen's parent, and you should leave the parenting of him to his parents. You seem to forget that you hated her as much as I did for all the lies and all the shit she has pulled and done to Kasen and our family.

Yes, maybe she has changed in your eyes, but I have changed as well. The only difference is that you are giving her the chance to show you she has changed without giving me that same chance.

51

I did not want to talk through email, but since you will not meet with me in person, I feel this is the best way to communicate with you.

Sincerely,

Travis

That night, I put my kids to bed, picked up the phone, and called him — something I never would have done in the past. I was ready to confront him. I wanted to hear his answers. In my opinion, this letter was carefully crafted. I touched on every point of his letter, but he kept going in circles. He had made up his mind. He sincerely believed I was never there for him, ever. I told him I hadn't seen or heard from him in months, so I had no idea about his sobriety, and kudos to him for being sober. I also reminded him that the "night of the sleepover" I let Kasen call his mom because, first, due to COVID-19, Disney was closed, and they weren't allowed to go on their vacation that week and, second, Cindy's long-time boyfriend had just committed suicide two days earlier. If he wanted to call his mom, damn right I was going to let him call his mom. Cindy needed to hear from him as much as he wanted to hear her voice. I don't consider that "parenting," but to each their own.

After that phone call, I was left confused again. He was saying one thing but acting another. Again, he kept putting blame on everyone else and painting this picture that he was doing so well when his actions spoke differently. Addiction is the biggest mind game for everyone involved.

I also found it sad that he felt like "we didn't want to hear it anymore." I don't have enough hands to count the number of times I have sat on the phone and listened to him. The only time I ever asked him to "discuss it later" was when he was clearly under the influence. Have you ever tried to rationalize or find a solution to a problem when someone is under the influence? It doesn't work. So yes, there were times when I had no more energy to keep going around and around in circles with someone who was drunk. And at that time, every time I talked to him, he was under the influence.

It was crazy to me how he expected me to always listen to him with disregard for me and my time. But everything, for the past decade or more, had always been about him and his needs, so I guess it's not that crazy.

This was the first time I put my foot down and set a boundary: I will not meet with you. Truthfully, I don't believe he liked that I told him no. I had never told him no. So, instead of having a phone conversation like I initially asked for, he wrote me a letter to try to get back at me, like, "Oh yeah? You don't want to do things my way? Well let me see how I can hurt you."

I believe (again, this is *my* perception) that he wanted to meet with me in person so that he could try to sweet talk me back into believing him and being on his side so I wouldn't tell anyone about his relapse. He knew he wouldn't have the same power over the phone. When I took that power away from him, he lashed out.

After that phone call, the next several months went by uneventfully. I think I was still in shock from everything that had happened, and I prayed every day that he would find help. It hadn't been a year yet; I was certain he would hit rock bottom at some point.

Since things were relatively quiet — as in, we hadn't heard from Travis — and the uncertainty was still a dark, heavy cloud hanging over us, we decided we needed to see our own counselor. We were ready to work on ourselves in order to move on. And we wanted a professional to tell us that we weren't crazy.

It's hard to explain what it's like to have no communication with someone you love, and they are telling the family they are doing well, but then other people are saying things about them that are different. It literally makes you question every thought you have. You ask yourself, *Is he doing well? Is he manipulating the situation? If he is doing so well, why are people saying these things about him? Am I wrong for feeling like he is lying?* This is what can make you crazy — that there are no answers to these questions.

I could literally loop all these questions in my head for hours. But I will explain all the wonderful things I learned from my counselor in Part Two.

At the end of June, three hours before a scheduled presentation (we hadn't had a presentation in months), Mom got a call from Karen that Travis was missing. He had been missing for three days already, and Karen didn't know what to do. She also stated that she was fed up with his drinking, and, when he did return, she would ask him to get help. I felt like calling Karen and saying, "Oh, I thought alcohol wasn't the problem!" But that would have been an asshole move, and I'm not an ass.

Kasen was supposed to go back to Travis's house at 5 p.m. because Travis and Cindy had 50/50 custody. However, because Travis was missing, Karen called Cindy and asked her to keep Kasen for the next few days, which she did. This was a big deal because it was the first time we'd ever felt like Karen was willing to do something that would help Travis. As heartbreaking as it was to get that call from Karen, we were also hopeful that this was his rock bottom and he would finally get the help he needed.

Karen followed through, and, when he returned, Travis got an assessment and went through a virtual intensive outpatient program (IOP) [2] due to COVID. He, of course, passed with flying colors because he knew exactly what to say. He even reached out to Mom to let her know what his next steps were. But I'm proud of my mom. She didn't jump back into old habits and start checking in with him every day because that was not healthy for her. Though she did question whether he was sincere or not. She was changing, thanks to counseling, and I don't think he liked it at all. For the first time in his thirty-odd years, he was facing the natural consequences all by himself without his parents jumping in to rescue him — something I've been asking

2 IOP is the level of treatment after counseling, but before someone might go into residential treatment.

my parents to do for the past two decades at least, but who am I to tell them what to do?

We, once again, felt hope that this was it. Travis would finally stay sober, take ownership of his actions, and we could work to rebuild our relationships. He never made contact with me, and only a handful of times with my parents.

Then he went silent. Yet again.

Around this time, Cindy filed for full custody of Kasen. She had given Travis a whole year to get help, and, so far, he wasn't able to stay sober for more than a few weeks.

As we neared the year anniversary of the relapse, I really struggled. I struggled more this time than at any other time on this journey. I really felt that I had let it go and moved on, but, for some reason, it hit me hard, and I couldn't let go. I guess I spent the first year of his relapse floundering, waiting for him to hit rock bottom, then get help and get sober. And, so far, that had not happened. I had to face the reality that it might never happen. I can't tell you the number of tears I cried. Maybe it was because we lost so much with COVID that the loss of my brother weighed so heavily on me. I finally met with my counselor, Roxanne, and she really helped me. One of the things she wanted me to do was to journal my feelings, which I did. Here is an excerpt from my journal:

> I am HURT because he lied to me for three years. I trusted, believed, and defended him. I knew he was acting differently lately, but I totally missed the signs. I'm ANGRY because he just won't tell the truth, and his wife just covers it all up for him. I'm also BLESSED because letting go of my relationship with him has allowed me to grow in my other relationships. I'm SAD because my children don't have their uncle and I cannot see my niece. The craziest thing about all of this (and those who have lived or are living through this can understand) is that we can have all of these emotions IN ONE DAY. We call addiction a rollercoaster of emotions.

For those of you who are not living this, let me give you a scenario:

Things are going fine; you feel *detached* from the situation. Then you hear that, let's say, your child is coming home drunk every night, so you feel *angry* because you thought everything was going well. Then your mind starts all the questions: *Why is he drinking? Where is he drinking? Why are the people in his life not doing anything about it?* Then something happens where your child gets a consequence, so you feel *happy* because, *finally*, maybe he will get help. Then you hear that the consequence given was short-term, and he's figured out how to manipulate the system. You feel *shocked, confused,* then *sad* because you had your hopes up. Then you go back to being *angry* because he continues to do what he does. Then you *detach* yourself again and *hope* that the next day is better.

These emotional swings would keep me up at night. They also made me realize that, the more energy I spent on my brother, the less I had for my husband, my kids, and my life.

Part of my job at Your Choice to Live Inc. is to work with concerned others — mostly students in high school who are affected by alcohol and drug use, whether it's a parent or a sibling. One of the things that I have them do is to write a "dear addiction" letter. Well, it was about time I practiced what I preached. On August 27, 2020, a little over one year after I found out about the relapse, I sat outside on my front porch with a cup of coffee and a notebook. It was pouring rain, and I decided to write a goodbye letter to my brother. I think the reason I had been so sad was because I deeply missed him and the relationship we had. I had to put those feelings on paper. With a pen in my hand and tears flowing down my cheeks, I wrote this letter:

Dear Brother,

This is my goodbye letter to you. You've been gone

over a year now, and I miss you terribly. Even though you are still here in the physical world, the person who is here is not you. I miss having someone to hang out with, talk with, laugh with, and do stuff with the kids. You were so funny, quick-witted, and always available to help. I had lost you as a teen, but this time hurts worse because I'm not sure I will ever get my brother back. I grieve the loss of you every day, and, at times, it seems too much. I see something funny and reach for my phone to text you, but then I'm reminded that you are no longer here. Although my kids don't know that you are gone, I know one day they will ask. I will have to tell them that this vicious thing called addiction took you from them. I will tell them stories of how great you were. You loved cars and music. I have friends who have lost siblings, and they grieve every day for them. But grieving a sibling who's gone but still physically here is its own special hell. Even though the good memories of you are fading, I will always hope against hope that you will find your way back. You have a small space left in my heart, and I will leave it there for now. I love you. Until we meet again, goodbye.

After I wrote that letter, I closed my notebook and cried. For the first time in a year, I really grieved the loss of my brother.

Once I had composed myself, I decided to write a letter to the addiction that had taken my brother from me.

Dear Monster,

Welcome back you fucking asshole. I don't know who you are, but I HATE YOU. You pretend like you're perfect and have your shit together, but we all know deep down inside you are a coward too afraid to face the truth and show your weaknesses. The funny thing is, everyone can already see them. Yes, you are a master manipulator and even had the best of us fooled for years. But you slipped up, got sloppy, people found out, and we're not buying your bullshit anymore. The truth always comes out, and one day you will pay. I hope nothing bad happens to the children. Does lying give you a sense of power? What do you gain from it? If you would just be honest, this would all go away, but then everyone would see that you failed. The truth is we all fail, but not you; you seem to be superior to everyone else. You can keep on living your sad, miserable life because I'm done with it all. You are nothing to me. I am putting zero energy into you. I have way more important things and people in my life that need my full attention. I am not wasting a single second on a piece of shit coward who lies and only thinks of himself.

Acknowledging this angry part of me also helped me release the anger and hate I had inside me. I closed my notebook and felt a huge weight lifted off my chest. I addressed the two parts of Travis that were hurting me the most.

I didn't know it at the time, but this exercise helped me prepare for what was yet to come.

A week later, I received a phone call from Cindy that Travis was visibly drunk on the video call with Kasen. Kasen even asked his mom after the call if something was wrong with his dad. Mind you, he had just finished intensive outpatient treatment the week before with "flying colors." Since Cindy saw Karen sitting right next to Travis, she asked Karen to send her a breathalyzer result to verify that he had been sober and she got no response. Now, in my mind, if I was fighting to get my child back (Cindy still had Kasen) and I was sober, I would happily submit a breathalyzer anytime I was asked. But that's just my opinion.

Anyway, Cindy asked my mom or dad to give Travis a call to see if they could pick up anything in his voice. She wanted to verify that she wasn't going crazy or seeing something that wasn't there. My dad tried to call Travis, but he did not answer.

Ironically, the very next morning, Travis texted Mom and

said he wanted to talk to her but was afraid that "anything he said would be used against him in court." That text really put my mom in a tough place. On one hand, she would do anything to help him get sober and back to being healthy; on the other hand, if he was not sober, she wouldn't lie for him as she had so many times in the past. She also had to protect her grandson. She ended up texting him back that she would meet with him, but he didn't respond. Back to the cycle.

Two days later, the boys had football practice together, and Travis never showed. He had attended all other practices, and this was the first one he'd missed. Karen walked right up to me like nothing ever happened, and I got to see my niece, whom I hadn't seen in months, which was awesome. I should have asked Karen right then and there where Travis was, but, at that point in time, I hadn't really found my voice yet.

The next day, Mom got another text from Travis asking to meet. Once more we all got our hopes up that this was his breaking point and he was going to say he needed help. But no. She went over to his house, and he acted like nothing — and by nothing, I literally mean nothing — ever happened over the last year. It was damage control. He now had the pressure of the court on him, and he wanted to prove to the court that he had a relationship with his family.

Unfortunately, my mom did buy his bullshit at first; she didn't see it as damage control. She called me on her way home from his house and told me that he looked good and was doing well. But that didn't really match up with what I was hearing from Cindy, the text he sent to Mom the other day, or the way he looked at football practice when he did show up. So I started questioning her on parts of his story. We actually got into a fight over it, and I ended up hanging up on her, which is something I would normally never do to my mother.

Remember, I'd tried to get her to see his manipulation when he's using for over ten years when we were younger, so my frustration with these situations ran deep. I know for a fact I had some fear that Mom would return to her old ways and undo all the growth we've had in the past year.

Once things settled down a bit, Mom and I were able to have an honest conversation. The most frustrating part was how Travis knew just the right things to say to get Mom to question herself.

Let me give you some examples. At this most recent meeting, Travis told Mom that his mind races all the time and he just wants it to stop. That's why he drank in the past. Then my mom tells me, "He needs to meet with an ADHD doctor to get on some medication to help him." My response was, "He's known he's had ADHD since he was in third grade, so why, in the past year when he was supposedly seeing counselors and getting treatment, was this never addressed? Her response: "Good question." It's easy to fall into the trap of believing it's something else other than what it really is. She's a mom, and we moms want to believe our children and protect them at any cost.

Another thing that Travis kept saying to Mom is that we were only hearing Cindy's side of things and not his. But when we asked for his side, he had no response.

Cindy's side is one of the things I have looped about and really tried to take a step back from and look at from an outsider's perspective. Yet I always came back to wondering, *Why would she lie? What would she gain if she lied?* She wanted nothing more than for Travis to be sober and for us to have our family back together. Lying about what she saw from Travis gained her nothing.

Plus, I was the one that told her he was drinking. It came from me first. Travis also claimed that Cindy was a bad person, but a year ago he would sit with her at every game (when Karen wasn't around). They got along great, and he would check in on her every now and then. So what changed? How did it go from getting along great to her being a bad person? The only thing that changed was that he was caught drinking.

Travis, on the other hand, had every reason to lie. If he were to tell the truth, he could risk losing custody of his son. He seemed too prideful and, I would guess, full of shame to admit that he relapsed and was struggling to find sobriety.

These are the things I sometimes have to remind Mom of when she gets trapped in his manipulative lies. And if they actually aren't lies, then time will tell. But, so far, we've been right.

After meeting with mom, Travis felt pretty confident that he had pulled Mom back into believing his BS. He was confident that, if they went to court, she would say he was doing well. With his newfound confidence, he texted Mom every day over Labor Day weekend to see if she and Dad wanted to hang out. What Travis didn't know was that Mom had done a lot of work on herself and she could now see through the BS. She said no each time. It's not that she didn't want to see him again, it's just that she didn't want to fall into his trap or get her hopes up only to have them squashed. She wanted to spend the weekend collecting her own thoughts without the influence of him. If he genuinely *was* sober and doing well, he would respect her wishes.

Ten days later, Kasen shared with me that Travis had been getting home late at night and jumping in bed with him smelling like alcohol. He, again, wasn't showing up for practices either. Being on the outside and knowing the cycle, we knew that Travis's life was falling apart. But there was nothing we could do.

After hearing this information, Mom and I decided to meet with our counselor. We wanted to ask her (again) if we were crazy and if there was anything we could do, but we already knew the answers. She provided us with a great analogy about addiction and codependency (see Canoe in Part Two) which helped us both a lot. She also talked to us about setting boundaries, which we did.

Mom and I spent a few days reading about boundary setting and wrote our own boundaries for Travis. Throughout Travis's relapse, Mom always felt like she had to *do something*. After she wrote her boundaries, and with some help from our counselor, she decided to call Travis and share her boundaries with him.

Unfortunately, when she made the call, Travis was clearly inebriated. She couldn't even make out what he was saying, so she hung up. The next morning, she texted Karen and asked if it was time for an intervention. After hearing him inebriated, she again went into "mom fix-it mode."

I'm not kidding you, immediately after she sent that text, Travis called again. She was afraid to answer because she thought Karen had told him about the text. She answered anyway, and, unfortunately, he was inebriated and wanted to unleash on her.

In a way, hearing him inebriated was a relief. We had our suspicions, and we'd heard from a third party that he wasn't sober, but it could make us feel crazy when he was telling us the opposite. Confirming our suspicions made us feel less crazy. Plus, Mom wanted to hear or see it first-hand. If she had to go stand in front of a judge and tell her side of the story, she wanted to share first-hand experience, not hearsay.

A few hours later, Karen texted back "yes" regarding the intervention. We immediately jumped into rescue mode, and I called an interventionist. The interventionist said, since we didn't have a relationship with Travis at that time, an intervention as a family would not work. We would all sit at the meeting, tell Travis if he didn't change that he would lose his family, and Travis would say, "Good. Go." A failed intervention. There would be no reason to change. Karen would have to be the one to do the intervention. I gave Karen the interventionist's number and let her take it from there.

I also called Cindy to let her know that her suspicions were confirmed and Karen was ready for an intervention. She was relieved. Remember, the goal had always been to get Travis the appropriate treatment so that we could get our loving and kind brother, father, son, and husband back. She called the guardian ad litem to fill her in on the situation.

About ten minutes after I got off the phone with Cindy, my mom's phone rang and it was the guardian ad litem wanting to know what was going on. Mom was really apprehensive, still stuck between trying to get her son help while not wanting to hurt him and telling the truth. I am proud to say she went with the truth. She let her know what had happened and that we were hoping to do an intervention the next day. Our dream was to have all the players at the table so that Travis couldn't divide us, though that never happened. But the guardian ad litem immediately gave Cindy temporary primary placement.

After this whole whirlwind of a day, we heard nothing. I don't think any of us slept that night.

The next morning, I went to work and proceeded with my day as normal. Mom came into the office two hours later and told me she had met with Travis. She hadn't wanted to tell me that she was meeting with him because she didn't want to go into the meeting with anyone else's thoughts, suggestions or feelings in the back of her mind.

The first thing she noticed was a horrible rash on his face. When she asked him what happened, he said he fell off a roof. Then he said he was sick of lying and what really happened was that he was so inebriated, he fell out of his truck and hit the pavement. He also said that losing custody of his son, Kasen, was giving him the motivation to change — he was finally ready. She gave him numbers to call, wished him luck, and they parted ways.

Then we got a text from Karen that she wanted to meet. So she came into the office and said the last month had been super tough. She'd printed out divorce papers, he'd signed them, and, if he didn't sober up, she was filing them. She wanted to tell us what had been going on, but we told her it wasn't important. The last time she told us what was going on, we were the ones blamed, and, quite frankly, I didn't want to hear it. She did, however, say that Travis was disappointed that no one reached out to him when he completed IOP. We hadn't even *known* that he'd completed IOP. During every interaction that had taken place in the past month, Travis had been drunk or he'd just wanted to sweep everything under the rug, and we were not going to do that anymore.

Karen and I also talked about getting the kids together and possibly working on a relationship outside of Travis.

After that meeting, everyone felt better, like we were moving in the right direction. For the first time, there was an external source involved — the court. Maybe having them involved would finally drive Travis to get the help he needed. This was September 2020, thirteen months after we found out about the relapse.

October came and went with no incidents. Mom and Travis texted each other positive quotes a couple times a week.

I wish to God the story got better from here, but that is not the case.

Not even a month and half later, Cindy found out that Travis had filed a motion to review the temporary order of the guardian ad litem.

The following were listed in the motion:

• The guardian ad litem's modification of the schedule was based upon statements made to her by two individuals that lack any real knowledge as to my current living situation.

(Kasen was temporarily removed from Travis's care because Mom had told the GAL of the situation. Mom, at the time, was very aware of what was going on because she had met with both Karen and Travis.)

• I am estranged from these family members and they have not had personal knowledge of my affairs or daily living for over a year. Any information they are fed is from "Cindy" who also lacks any real personal knowledge as to my daily living environment.

(Interesting that he claimed this considering there had been numerous times Travis or Karen had met with Mom to discuss what had been going on — Travis going missing, needing an intervention, or his own admission of needing help. None of it included Cindy at all.)

• Essentially, the order was made based upon unsubstantiated hearsay by family members that are given unreliable information from "Cindy" but have not had any real contact or witnessed me in my daily life in well over a year.

(How could he say that when it was so far from the truth?)

• I believe that, given my estrangement with my family members, they are not being truthful as to my current circumstances with the guardian ad litem.

(Why on earth did we have had any reason to lie? We were "estranged" from him because of his drinking and inability to tell the truth.)

• They have motivation to be untruthful to the GAL due to the family conflict and their perceptions of our estrangement.

(I would have loved to have known the motivation. This had been absolutely tragic for our family. To say that we had motivation to be untruthful hurt.)

• These individuals have alleged statements from my wife to them, however, my wife has not made such statements.

(I wish Travis had been there when his wife came to our office asking for help. But proof of these "alleged statements" was available by reading text messages between Karen and my mom and me.)

• The guardian ad litem has not properly vetted the allegations and has not been in contact with my wife, who can substantiate or refute any and all claims against me.

(Again, these were easily verified by text messages.)

• I do not believe that I have been allowed a fair opportunity to address the allegations made against me prior to the guardian ad litem making the order, or since that time, for that matter.

(There was enough evidence to make the decision she did. I'm sorry that he didn't get time to try to manipulate the situation. Placement was removed in September, so why did he wait two months to file this motion?)

• I proposed an appropriate solution to alleviate everyone's alleged concerns and verify that no issues exist. This proposal was supposed to go in effect three weeks ago but, due to inaction, has not taken place, and I am being deprived of important placement time and connection with our son, which is detrimental to his well-being.

(His "appropriate solution" was to take a breathalyzer test every day at 1 p.m. and send the results to Cindy. However, the breathalyzer device was purchased six months prior and had yet to be used. Plus, having a set time to give a sample would have allowed him to start drinking at 1:01 p.m. and sober up by 12:59 p.m. the next day.)

• I believe the guardian ad litem's modification of placement schedule was made in error based upon the un-credible evidence from estranged family members who have an agenda against me.

(I wish everything that happened was made up. But it was not. And it was hurtful to make these claims.)

I seriously did not make this up. This was probably the most shocking thing I'd ever read in my entire life. How the hell did this happen? This was so far in left field from the discussions and conversations that happened less than two months prior, and to say that this was heartbreaking for me and my mom would be an understatement. We felt that hope we had in September slip away.

I was so sick of Travis and Karen walking all over us and getting away with it. I thought back to the conversation with Karen in September when she had mentioned getting the kids together. So I texted her, "Hello! When we got together at the end of September, you said you wanted to get the kids together more, and, since football is done, we would like to see Maggie. So I'm wondering if you have any time in the next couple of weeks to get the kids together. Let me know!"

I did really want to see Maggie, but another part of me wanted to see how she would respond, if at all. I was curious whether she would deny meeting with me at the end of September. Her response: "Absolutely! When I get home, I will check my calendar."

Huh? That was not at all the response I was expecting, and now I had to go through with it. We picked a date, they came over, and she was very surface level. Looking back, I should have asked how things were going with Travis, but I figured it would be a waste of breath since she wouldn't tell me the truth anyways. She even texted me afterwards saying that sledding should be our next adventure. Seemed strange she would want to hang out with an estranged family member with an agenda!

To be honest, after they left, I felt dirty. It didn't feel right to me. It was almost like she was playing with me. Though, admittedly, I was playing with her to see if her accusations were true. I was really pissed at the stuff they'd said in the motion. Yet I also had high hopes that she would've been honest and told me what was really going on.

A week later, at the motion hearing, Travis and Karen told the judge that Travis only drank once at the end of June and immediately went into IOP and hadn't drank since. They said the allegations my mom and I made were because he was trying to leave the family and we didn't want him to. According to him, we made up this elaborate story. They claimed that when Karen met with us in September, it was to try to get the family back together, not because of Travis's drinking problem.

If the motion was the knife in the back, these statements were the twist to drive it in deeper. After I heard this, my emotions were all over the place. I felt betrayed — not really by Travis because I was coming to expect this from him, but more so by Karen. Whenever she would come to us for help, we were there for her. How she could turn around and lie like this was so beyond me. The saddest part about the whole thing was that this would hurt her more than us in the long run. I told my mom, if she ever reaches out again, don't take her calls. I was so hurt by this that once the kids went to bed, I sat on my bathroom floor and cried. I secretly wished Travis would die. Not because I actually wanted him to die, but because I wanted this all to be over. We'd already lived this journey and I did not want to live through it again.

After my emotions were back in check, I realized how sick he really was — how sad, lonely, and ashamed he must be. He was protecting his secret at all costs, and his wife was there to help him.

Since I'd made the decision earlier to no longer sit back and keep my mouth shut, I texted Karen.

"I was shocked to hear that you are denying coming to us in September because you'd had enough of Travis's drinking and were looking for advice. If this is true, then you are keeping him sick. I welcomed you into my house to hopefully start a new chapter and at least let the kids have a relationship. But I will not continue if things are based on a lie."

She texted back,

"No questions have been asked to me, so how can I be denying anything?"

I replied,

"I read the motion."

I have not heard from her since.

Her response made me wonder if she'd even read that motion. Maybe Travis and his lawyer filed it without her knowing. But I highly doubt that. The little bit of sympathy I'd felt for her was completely gone. She was completely on her own now.

Not only was this betrayal a huge shock to me, but to my parents as well. To have hope, to hear directly from him that he needed help and wanted help, and then to get slapped in the face again was such a huge blow. But since we'd been doing so much work on ourselves, we were better equipped for the blow, though it didn't make it easier.

The addiction, lies, and betrayal were weighing on me one night, and I'm sure the kids could tell something was up. I was putting my youngest to bed (she was six at the time), and, while reading her a book, she asked if I had any siblings. I said, "I have one brother, and his name is Travis." And she said, "I hope one day I get to meet him." This struck me hard. This was now affecting my children. The good memories of my brother were starting to fade away, and they no longer remembered their uncle.

The next day was Travis's birthday. Instead of sending him a fake "happy birthday" text, I sent one from my heart. As tears streamed down my face, I texted these words to him:

"Yesterday, Tenley asked me if I had any siblings. I told her yes, I have a brother. She asked me what his name is, and I said Travis. She asked when she was going to meet him, and I said hopefully one day. With that said, my hope for your 34th year of life is that you find your inner peace and realize that we've only ever wanted what's best for you. And hopefully one day Tenley can meet 'my brother.' Happy Birthday."

No response.

A few weeks later, it was Christmas — our second Christmas without him. Since last Christmas went so well, we were all relaxed and excited to spend a drama-free Christmas together. Despite everything that had been going on, my kids wanted to make their cousin, Maggie, Christmas cards. And they picked out a gift, a book about cousins. Since Mom had also bought Maggie gifts, I gave these things to her to drop off. She texted both Travis and Karen that she was in the area and she would like to drop off the gifts. She could leave them on their front porch or she could stop by at a different time when they were home. No response. So she left them on their porch.

The day after Christmas, Mom got a call from my grandma. Grandma was sad because Travis stopped by and said he had no family and we were horrible people. My mom hadn't told Grandma everything that'd been going on because she's older and, quite frankly, doesn't need to know. Mom let her know that what he said was not true, keeping it simple with her so as to not upset her more.

After having the courage to have a voice with Karen, I decided to let Travis know that if he had issues with me, then he could talk to me, not take it out on our poor old grandma. But I also didn't want to throw Grandma under the bus, so I kept my message light. I sent him this message:

"If you have an issue with me or think I'm talking bad about you, you are more than welcome to come to me directly. I've moved on with my life and have no problem discussing any lingering issues you still have with me. And I hope Maggie enjoyed the gifts the kids picked out for her."

No response.

One week later, Mom received this text from Travis: "..."

Mom did not respond. A week later, she got another text asking for the presents. Not wanting to play his games, she did not respond. Kasen had already received the presents that Mom and Grandma had purchased when we'd celebrated Christmas together.

One month after Christmas is Maggie's and my birthday. My kids made cards for her. We bought her presents, and so did my mom. Once again, my mom texted:

> "Grandma informed me that there are presents she bought for Maggie and Kasen. It seems we only have presents for Maggie that you dropped off. As we don't want to be unfair to the kids, Maggie isn't going to open hers until she can do it with Kasen. Kasen is here until 3pm today, but won't be returning until Tuesday. How would you like to proceed? Only reason I ask is because I would like to have the kids thank Grandma for the presents together."
>
> "

This was the response she got from Travis:

> "Here is where I am with you guys seeing my daughter.
>
> I have always said you guys can see the kids whenever you like despite your relationship with me. You have chosen not to, and Maggie doesn't know a life with you. To start now would be fine IF I knew it would be consistent. Maggie does not need presents; she needed your presence as grandparents.
>
> Maggie has been affected enough not seeing her brother, and then seeing him, and then not again. It hurts her, and I do not want to do that to her.
>
> It's not to say I don't want you guys around, but with you still thinking I am actively using or engaging in

addictive behavior, despite the evidence I am not, I don't want the negativity in my life or around my family.

I have presents for Maggie, I can drop off tomorrow morning or dad and I can stop by tomorrow when she is home and personally give them to her. Please let me know what works best for you."

Shock was the first word that came to mind. One month prior, he'd repeatedly asked for the presents. Now he didn't want any? And we felt sorry that Maggie wasn't able to see her brother — it was heartbreaking, but we did not do that to them. The courts removed Kasen because of Travis's drinking. That was done because of his choices, but he blamed us for it.

Throughout his whole relapse, we hoped, prayed, and cried for him to be sober. Most of the time we didn't know either way. When people would ask us about him, we would say we didn't know how he was doing as we hadn't heard from him in a while.

Mom finally decided enough was enough. That text was meant to dig at her, and she was done tiptoeing around him. Here is the text string that followed:

Mom: I agree with your thoughts regarding Maggie. Whether you are sober or not is on you. I have moved past the drinking but am unable to move past the lies. Is it true that you are denying meeting me at Roots in September?

Travis: No that is not true. I have not denied meeting you at Roots.

Mom: So you are not denying that you were drinking in September and met with me for help?

Travis: (No response.)

Mom (two days later): Your silence speaks volumes. This is not about your drinking; this is about the lies as we both know the truth about what happened that week of our conversation we had at Roots. This is why I am choosing not to have a relationship with you, because I can't live with your lies. I hope one day you will tell Maggie the truth of why we are not in your life.

One week later, she received this:

"My silence is out of respect. Instead of reacting and saying something foolish, I'd rather compile my thoughts and respond accordingly.

I have not done anything but respect your wishes by not talking about court or bringing you into it. I also have not lied to you about anything. It's really hard to lie when you're not asked a question.

I can only assume the source[3] of the information that is leading you to believe I'm lying. All I can do is urge caution, but that is something you have all known before but forgotten.

I realize that it is much easier to believe that I am lying or using or whatever else you choose to brand me with. What you fail to realize is that I can handle it because I've lived with being your failure my entire life.

It's sad the way things turned out. But, as you always say, everything happens for a reason. It would have taken a phone call and conversation to clear things up. It would have taken a mother being a mother, not judge, jury and executioner.

As Chris (Travis's sponsor) keeps telling me, the truth always wins. On that day, try not to hate yourself too much. Maggie will know why you're not in my life or her life, but she will know the truth.

I wish you all the best life you deserve. Enjoy everything you have all worked so hard to accomplish.

(I do not wish to continue going back and forth. It is pointless and tiring. So please, do not respond.)

3 Refers to Cindy

What a blow! That text was meant to directly hurt my mother. The things he said were so untrue, but those were his truths, and he had to live with them. If you asked anyone who had been close with us during this relapse, they would have told you how painful it had been for all of us.

That was the last communication my mom, dad, or I have had with Travis.

The court case ended with fifty/fifty custody between Cindy and Travis.

Travis was not happy with that and filed a motion with 104 bullet points as to why he should have full custody of his son. *Yes, you read that right! 104 bullet points.* The case is going to trial.

By this time, we had started to work harder on ourselves. We began enjoying the lives we had right in front of us but had been ignoring because we were so caught up in trying to help Travis. We knew there was absolutely nothing more we could do.

Looking back at this two-year journey of relapse, I can see so much growth — not only in myself, but in my parents. My story — our story — is far from over, but if I had the chance to say anything to him right now, I would say, "Thank you. Thank you for helping me get out of the shadows."

Introduction

A s I revisit the past and experience the challenges I am going through today, I see patterns. Patterns that, even in the recovery stage, repeated themselves. Aside from the family therapy in treatment, we had never really worked on ourselves. We were a boundary-less, codependent family that lived every day walking on eggshells just to avoid something more tragic than what was already going on.

Addiction is a disease unlike any other. It is one of the few diseases where the person who is sick cannot see their illness. And, oftentimes, when they do recognize they have a problem, they don't want to acknowledge it. For some, they will do anything in their power to hide their addiction at all costs.

However, those who are around that person can see it clear as day. Despite our best efforts, we cannot love someone into recovery. Many parents, siblings, spouses, children, grandparents, aunts, uncles, cousins, and friends have spent countless hours worrying about their loved one, praying deeply that they will get help. And still the loved one with substance use disorder chooses the substance over them.

My story isn't anything special. Some of you probably have a similar story. I am also not anyone special. I am a basic girl who loves animals, kids, and being outside.

This second part of this book is designed to help those who are living this nightmare. My goal is to let you know you are not alone and to give you some ideas on how to move forward with your life. For those of you who aren't in this position, hopefully this brings to light the challenges addiction creates for families.

The Shadow Child

"In a position of being unnoticed because
all the attention is given to someone else."
— Merriam-Webster

For many years, I've been sharing my story of what it's like to be a sibling of someone with substance use disorder. I would talk about the teenage years and all the challenges we faced as a family. Then I'd talk about what it was like to get my brother back once he found recovery, giving so many families hope that they would one day experience what I had.

Even though my story at the time brought others hope, I had this feeling. I couldn't quite put a name to it until Travis relapsed, then I began working on myself, digging deep, and looking at how my life had played out over the last thirty-plus years. That's when I realized I'd been living in my brother's shadow for almost my entire life.

When Travis was born, he came out feisty. He was the type of child that always demanded your attention. Being the older, quiet, less needy child, I never fought for more attention.

As Travis got older, he became very charismatic, and people loved him. I never had to worry about filling silence because Travis was always cracking jokes. If I was nervous about going somewhere new, Travis would come with me. He always knew the right things to say, and the attention was never on me.

Even when Travis was using substances, all the focus was on him. At school, I was known as "the drug addict's sister," not Ashleigh, which, at the time, was fine. I wasn't outgoing or charismatic. I was introverted and really didn't mind flying under the radar.

When Travis got sober and his outgoing, fun, charismatic side returned, the persona of being "just Travis's sister" remained. He was the one who was going to tell his story and change the world. I felt like Your Choice to Live Inc. *needed* him to be at every presentation because he was the one people wanted to hear. It didn't matter that I had my own story or that I did everything behind the scenes — the marketing, website design, accounting, literally everything else. He was the star of the show.

I was okay with it. I never wanted to be in the spotlight, preferring to remain in the background. Plus, that's how it had been my entire life, why change it now?

Too afraid to come out of the shadows, I had lost my voice. I never really thought anyone cared what I had to say or what I felt. If I did come out of the shadows, I would be exposed. I was afraid that people would never like me as much as they liked my brother. So I remained silent for many years after Travis found sobriety.

I found out about my brother's relapse one month before presentation season was scheduled to begin. Not only did Travis tell his story, but he was the opener and closer of our student presentations. I honestly thought, *How the hell are we going to pull this off without him? There is no way in hell I can do what he did.*

I remember sitting in my office at work discussing with my mom what we were going to do with all the student presentations we had booked for the fall. Because the relapse was so recent and she believed him when he said that he only drank once and quit, she wanted him to continue. But I was adamant that he no longer speak for Your Choice, at least for the foreseeable future. I decided that I would take over his opening and closing. We didn't need him. I had been presenting on stages for almost ten years. I could do this.

Was it scary as hell? Yes. Did I do it the same as him? No. But I did it *my* way. We actually had one of the best presentation seasons we've ever had. The feeling that we *needed* him started to fade away.

As time went on, our programs at Your Choice started to evolve without Travis. I realized that, while his story was and is still important, my story and my expertise are just as important. Many people that know Your Choice today don't even know Travis or his story.

And as I began to gain confidence at work, I started to see it leaking into my personal life as well. People really *did* like me for me, not because I was someone's sister. Sure, I felt exposed. I didn't have someone to lean on to take over the conversation when I felt scared. But it felt much better than being a voiceless person living in someone else's shadow.

If you are like I was and living in someone else's shadow, you can find your way out. It doesn't need to be a big leap. Start small. Do something you've never done before, and do it by yourself. You can and will fail, but remember, it's temporary. You can learn from it and pick yourself back up. *You are just as important as everyone else.*

Sibling Roles in Addiction

"In a time of distress and change, we may cling all the more to family roles that have worked for us in the past. Instead, we can learn to let go. We can learn new patterns of behaviour."
— Katerine T. Owen

When a sibling suffers from substance use disorder, the other siblings take on different roles. Some become an enabler, others become the scapegoat, while others are the lost child.

There is a lot of research out there to describe all the different roles people take on when someone in the family is addicted to substances.

I definitely took on the role of the hero. An online article, "6 Common Family Roles in an Addicted Households," defines the family hero as "your typical Type-A personality: a hard-working, overachieving perfectionist. Through his or her own achievements, the hero tries to bring the family together and create a sense of normalcy. This role is usually taken on by the eldest child, as they seek to give hope to the rest of the family. Unfortunately, a driving need to 'do everything right' tends to put an extreme amount of pressure on the hero, leaving them highly anxious and susceptible to stress-related illnesses later in life" (2019). This definition describes me to a T. But I do recognize this about myself and work every day to not pressure myself to be perfect.

Another role that we, as siblings, take on that isn't talked about much is the role of a caregiver. Our parents are obviously and understandably deeply affected by their child's addiction. All of their focus and attention is on that child.

Meanwhile, the other children not only have to take care of themselves emotionally because our parents' emotions are focused elsewhere, they also start to carry the emotions of their parents. When Mom is sad, the siblings comfort her even though they may be sad as well. It's almost like we put our feelings aside to help our parents navigate our sibling's addiction.

I think we are often stuck in the middle. Siblings can sometimes be our best friends, plus many children care deeply for their parents. So when our sibling is struggling, they reach out to us and we try to help. Then we also try to help our parents. Oftentimes, we don't have anyone to talk to about how we feel about the situation — there is no outlet for us. Obviously, our sibling doesn't want to hear it, and how could we possibly burden our parents? They have enough going on. So we bury our feelings and go on through life. Then those emotions creep up in subtle ways.

As I've been working on myself, I've noticed that, during times of turmoil, I don't know what I'm feeling. For example, the other day, Travis did something that really hurt my mom and me. While discussing it with our counselor, she asked me, "What feeling or emotion does this bring up for you?" I sat there, searching inside for an answer. And I couldn't find one. I could not for the life of me pinpoint what I was feeling.

For so many years, no one ever asked how I was feeling. I was always so concerned about everyone else's feelings that my feelings got buried deep inside of me. To actually look inside and find the hurt is one of the things I have to work on — where does it hurt, and how does it hurt? — then allow myself to feel it.

If you are a parent reading this, please take what I have shared into consideration. Maybe your child seems cold about the situation, but are they just repressing their feelings to protect you? How much are you leaning on your children for help? Would it be better to lean on your therapist/best friend/ support group and not put it all on the other kids?

For those siblings out there like me, I feel you. We take on more than we have to at times. But we will be okay.

Anticipatory Grief

"Expecting is the greatest impediment to living.
In anticipation of tomorrow, it loses today."
— Lucius Annaeus Seneca

For those of us who have someone important in our lives that is struggling with substance abuse, it's not only the fear of them dying, but it's anticipating the next blowup, fight, phone call, or crisis.

For the first year of Travis's relapse, my parents and I were always waiting for the next thing to happen or, as they say, the other shoe to drop. When was the next phone call going to be that he was drunk, in trouble, missing, or not showing up to things? We lived in this vicious cycle, and it felt like there was no way out.

Then I learned about anticipatory grief. Anticipatory grief refers to a feeling of grief occurring before an impending loss.

Living in this fear or anticipation of something happening is hell. You wake up in the morning thinking, *Today is going to be a good day,* then you think, *But he could die,* or, *What do I do if I get a call that he needs help?,* or, *If he doesn't get help, something is going to happen.* This cycle might not happen every day, but when something does happen, it starts the cycle over, and it can last a few weeks.

About the time that I learned this term, I saw a post in a Facebook group I am part of, and it really hit home with me:

Today I had to say goodbye to my son who is still living! I can't emotionally stay on this rollercoaster! I try and try, and when he doesn't get what he wants then the hateful words come each time with more anger and hurt! I had to pretend to call the police for him to leave my house. I should have actually called! I blocked him on social media and his phone. I have never felt the need or want to not speak to my child before! I feel like I am mourning his death and he is still on this earth! I fear it won't be long before he actually isn't! I am lost and broken once again! As I sit here with tears rolling down my face, all I can do is keep telling myself it is OK to not communicate with him during this drug-induced rage and hate he turns towards me and his family! I pray for the families that continue to go through this pain I am going through. I now give it to the Lord! May he watch over our loved ones affected with this illness and guide them to a healthier journey in life! Amen

– Unknown

While I don't know what it's like as a mom to turn a child away, I feel like I could have written this post myself, riding the rollercoaster and waiting for something bad to happen.

They call addiction a rollercoaster because it's just like the real thing. You climb this steep hill anticipating the fall, which is the worst part for me. Once I start falling, I'm fine because it's what I expected. This is what was happening for me with my brother. I was anticipating the climb because I knew we would eventually fall.

Let me give you an example. It had been almost a year since we found out that Travis had been drinking again. Neither of my parents had seen or heard from him much. For the whole football season, he would attend every practice on his placement nights. He would tell people that he's doing good, just completed IOP, and life couldn't be better. We all thought, *Okay, that's awesome. I'm glad he's doing well.* Then I got the call and learned he was visibly drunk on video chat (start climbing the hill). Then he stopped showing up to practice (climb even higher). Then my nephew told me that his dad and stepmom were fighting all the time, and his dad was climbing into bed with him at 1:00 a.m. smelling like alcohol (keep climbing even higher, wondering if we will ever get to the top so we can make our way down).

The climb of this particular rollercoaster lasted just over a month until his wife finally agreed that he needed an intervention and further help. The whole time we were climbing this hill anticipating the drop, we were wondering if there was anything we could do. Was there something we could say or do to make the fall happen sooner before someone got hurt? And the answer: *No.*

I explained to my counselor that I learned the term "anticipatory grief," and how it really resonated with me. I'd been living my life in this anticipation for almost a year, and I was sick of it. No matter how much I worried about him or helped when Karen called, nothing was changing. They went on with their lives doing whatever they do, and I was left worrying about what was next.

My counselor, Roxanne, advised me to accept that this is how it will always be — he may never get sober, and I may never have a relationship with him. I had to stop focusing on *his* outcome because I have no control over that. It totally makes sense, and to anyone reading this, you're probably thinking *duh — I could have told you that for free.* But when you are living it, it is difficult to see clearly. Your emotions take over, and it's hard to be logical. Today, it's clear to me, but two years ago, it was hard not to anticipate something happening because it always did.

While working through my anticipatory grief, I also learned about "compounded grief," or grief on top of grief. Not only was I experiencing anticipatory grief, but I was also going through the loss of the relationship with my brother, the loss of the relationship with my niece, and loss of hope that I would ever have a relationship with them again. Add to that COVID and all the uncertainty with that — my kids were now virtually learning, there was much uncertainty with the virus — and I was dealing with a lot.

I was also grieving for my kids. The uncle that they knew and loved was no longer there for them. While they may not have seen it or felt it in the beginning, they are definitely feeling it now. The last time I physically saw my brother, which was five months after the last communication he had with our mom, he was coming out of football gear pick-up. It was the first year the boys — my son and his son — were playing tackle football. While Ryan and Nolan went in to get fitted for football pads, Teagan, Tenley, and I waited in the car. As we were waiting for them to return, we saw Travis, Kasen, Cindy, and her boyfriend Chase walk out of the gym. The girls wanted to say hi so they jumped out of the car and ran towards them. Travis did not acknowledge them at all. Teagan was so hurt that Travis couldn't even say hi that she asked me if she even has to call him uncle, to which I replied, "No." My heart broke for them. I had been anticipating this for the past two years, not knowing how he would handle my kids.

Throughout all this, I haven't told my kids much. When they ask where their uncle is, I say, "He's busy." When they ask why he doesn't call during the holidays or wish them a happy birthday, I say, "Maybe he forgot." Recently, they were asking so many questions that I finally said that he was making poor choices, that I was concerned for his safety so I had to tell Kasen's mom about the choices he was making, and for that he was angry at me. All of it is the truth. So when he walked by them, completely ignoring them, they still didn't understand why he couldn't just say hi. To be completely honest, I don't understand it either. They didn't do anything, and they don't deserve to be treated like that. Yet at the same time, I do feel some relief — relief that my kids can grieve the loss of the relationship with their uncle and move on, relief that he's not going to be in and out of their lives.

While working through all this grief with my counselor, she told me to recognize these losses and know that they will come and go. We'll grieve and move on, but then something will remind us — an anniversary, holiday, birthday, smell, or a quote — and that grief will come back. And that's okay. It doesn't mean we are not healthy. We just have to recognize the grief, grieve it, and pick ourselves back up.

I think of all the families we have worked with, and I can't think of one that has not experienced both of these types of grief. No matter how involved or not a person is in someone's life, we worry about or anticipate what is going to happen if that loved one does not get help.

The same thing goes with compounded grief. When a loved one gets addicted, we don't just grieve the loss of them as we knew them, but we may grieve the loss of relationship with their spouse, children, etc.

If you are in the thick of it right now, know you are not alone. While it may be easy for someone to tell you to *get over it*, I know it's not that easy. You want that relationship back, you want them healthy, and you'll do just about anything to help them, even if it means worrying yourself sick.

But also know that you don't have to be sick. Yes, something will happen — good or bad. When you live your life worrying about someone else, you miss out on your own life. How many sleepless nights does your loved have thinking about how *their* choices affect *you*? Unfortunately, as part of the disease, they are only focused on themselves and what feels good to them. Recognize your grief, grieve it, and start living your life.

The Codependency Canoe

"Make sure everybody in your boat is rowing
and not drilling holes when you're not looking."
—Unknown

Early on in our journey, both Mom and I struggled with helping Travis. Should we help him? If so, *how* so? Was there even anything we could do to help him? And our wonderful counselor said, "You are stuck in the codependency canoe."

Codependency is "a relationship in which one person is psychologically dependent in an unhealthy way on someone who is addicted to a drug or self-destructive behavior." Now, some will argue that codependency is not a real thing, and others believe it is. Whether or not codependency is "real," those of us living in this space can either see the attachment that others have, say mom and son, or we *are* the attached person. There is no denying that there is something pulling us towards that person.

So when a loved one clearly needs help but they want nothing to do with you, what do you do? For years they've been your emotional support and you've been theirs. Then something happens and you know they need help, but they deny having a problem and turn their back on you. Then when they do want help, you come running, and once you've done what you could, they turn on you. And once again, you're stuck.

To help both my mom and me understand addiction and codependency, our counselor shared this canoe analogy with us:

Imagine you are in a boat and your loved one, who is abusing substances, is drowning. You don't want to pull them into the boat because, if you do, you know they still won't stop using substances. But you don't want them to drown, so every once in a while you pull them up by their hair and give them a breath of air — giving them money, food, a ride, etc. As long as you keep giving them that air, they don't need to change. Meanwhile, the boat is creeping towards Niagara Falls. If you stay with that person, eventually you will fall over the cliff with them. So you have two choices: pull them back in the boat, or throw them a life vest and row away. You know you can't pull them back in the boat with you because their addiction will consume you again. By rowing away, it's up to them to save themselves. If they have been able to find a way to get drunk or high, they can find a way back to shore.

This analogy really helped both Mom and me. When Travis was a teen, my mom (my dad didn't know) would bail him out of everything — jail, school, or tight money situations. Every time she did that, she pulled him back into our canoe. Every time he was in our canoe, he was angry, rude, and destructive, and our family suffered. After ten years of dragging his ass back into the canoe and nothing changing, they kicked him out. But two weeks later, they threw a life jacket out there for him to go to treatment, which he did. He used the lifejacket to swim to shore and get himself help.

With the recent relapse, we originally pulled him in the boat (old habits die hard), but he kept falling out. No matter how much we tried to help, he kept drinking, giving us an excuse every time for why it was ok that he drank. A friend of ours at the time, who was in long-term recovery himself and happened to be a counselor, said to us, "You cannot rescue him. You have to let him figure this out on his own." It was so early in his relapse when we heard this advice, and we had not yet begun to work on ourselves, that I don't think we fully understood what he meant. So we took the advice and stuck it in our back pockets.

On the day that he was caught drinking at work, we got the call from his wife that the alcohol wasn't the problem, we, his family, were the problem. That day, we made the decision to leave him. We took our canoe and rowed to shore. If we were the problem, then removing ourselves from his life would allow him to swim back to shore and have a wonderful life. We were no longer going to rescue him.

That was, until his wife called for help eight months later when Travis went missing. Mom, Dad, and I had been working on ourselves at shore and had not had much communication with Travis at all. When Karen came to Mom asking for help, my mom did what most moms would do. She got back in her canoe, rowed to the drowning Travis, pulled him up for air, and gave him a life jacket, offering all the help and support she could. While Travis and Karen might deny it to this day, when we left Travis eight months prior, Travis never made it to shore. He continued to struggle with his addiction. Us leaving him did not solve his drinking problem. *Are you surprised?* I'm not.

Since us leaving Travis's life didn't cure him of his drinking problem, Karen got into her codependency canoe, rowed out to him, and pulled him in. When she could no longer handle him being in her canoe, she threw him out and called Mom to bring the life jacket. Then Mom came rowing along with the life jacket. As soon as Travis got the life jacket, he didn't swim to shore. No, he used it to swim back into his wife's canoe. The cycle continued until Mom had had enough. Over time, Mom learned that pulling him up for air or giving him a lifejacket only makes her hurt more, and does nothing for him but keep him sick.

For me specifically, this analogy really helped me understand why my mom does what she does, and it helped me understand her better. My dad and I stayed at shore and never went back to rescue him. We knew when we left that day that he was going to have to figure it out on his own. Nothing we could say or do would help him.

I will admit, in the beginning, there were times when I pulled out my binoculars and looked for him just to see if he was still alive. I would drive by his house to see if he was home or go home a certain way just for the chance that I would see him driving his truck. I needed the peace of mind that he was still alive.

But as time went on and I worked on healing myself, it became easier to let him go. When I found out about the motion that was filed right after he asked Mom for help the final time, I vowed I would never, ever take my boat out again. The fact that someone could ask for help, crying that they could no longer go on, wanting to rebuild the relationship, and then turn around and call us vindictive liars was something that I just could not understand. That day, I burned my canoe. Travis and Karen were on their own this time no matter how big the problem became.

With all the families I've met and worked with over the past twelve years, I see this cycle repeating over and over. I'm fortunate that Travis did file that motion because it was a closure for me, and I would say my mom, too, that most people don't get. If Travis and Karen had not done that, I believe my mom would've continued to reach out to him and try to pull him up for air. Travis and Karen would've remained at the edge of the waterfall because they knew that they had someone they could rely on. By us cutting off all communication with them, even though it's hard because there are kids involved, hopefully they are finding their own way. Hopefully they are working together to get to shore without relying on other people to help them out when they are drowning.

But, for families that are not as fortunate to have the closure we did, it's easy to think, *I have to help this time because this could be the time that they get help.* Meanwhile, other family members could be thinking, *You've been helping them for five years and nothing's changed! When will you learn*? And then the family starts fighting about who's right and who's wrong as the person who needs helps just keeps doing what they do.

My advice (while it may not be the right fit for your family) is to first look at how each family member handles the cry for help. Does Mom jump in to help, Dad get angry and turn away, and the siblings get stuck in the middle? Then, try to understand where each other is coming from. Is one person more codependent than the other? How can you help that person? Then take a step back and look at what you've done in the past. Has it helped? Lastly, talk to a counselor or therapist about breaking free from the codependency canoe if you've tried everything and nothing is working.

I think one of the scariest parts of our journey was to put our foot down and say, "We can no longer help you." But it's also been one of the most helpful steps in our own journey. We know we tried everything we could, and we are at peace with the fact that he has to figure it out on his own. We've seen success with this in many other families. When they let go, they got stronger, which in turn helps the struggling person grow, however painful it may be.

Boundaries

"Boundaries are a part of self-care.
They are healthy, normal, and necessary."
– Doreen Virtue

When your loved one is addicted, you want to fix them and tell them what they need to do to get help. But, in most cases, the success is minimal. That's where boundaries come in.

Boundaries were one of the first things our counselor, Roxanne, had my mom and me learn about and develop for ourselves.

She told us we had no boundaries with Travis, and it would help us tremendously to set them. Obviously, my first thought was, *I do have boundaries: 'I don't want to talk to you until you get sober.'* Simple. Easy. Done. What's next?

Well, it's not that easy. The definition of a boundary is "a line that marks the limits of an area; a dividing line."[4] Think about it as a fence around your yard with a gate. You let the good in and keep the bad out.

Roxanne pointed out that boundaries are not meant to change the other person — you have no control over what they do. They are set to protect yourself, kind of like a list of what you are willing to do and not do. Here are some examples:

4 Lexico.com, s.v. "boundary," accessed October 15, 2021, https://www.lexico.com/en/definition/boundary.

• If you are angry, that's okay. But I'm choosing to walk away until things settle down.

• You can drink if you choose, but not in my house.

• I will not lie for you in court.

At first, this was a hard concept. How do you set a boundary for someone you want to change?

Roxanne emailed me some great reading materials, and I quickly began working on my boundaries with Travis. Here are the boundaries I set one week prior to Travis reaching out to our mom for help:

Changes being implemented

I will not have any contact with you unless you take responsibility for your actions and do what you need to do to get healthy.

What I will do

• Pray

• Hold true to my boundaries

• Limit my children's interactions

• Always have Kasen's best interest in mind

What I will not do

• Lie in court

• Make excuses for your behavior

• Try to fix you — only you can fix yourself

My mom also set her own boundaries with Travis. Unlike her, I never felt the need to share mine with him. He hadn't reached out to me in months, and these were designed to keep me in check. When I questioned if I was doing something right, I would check in with my boundaries to find my answer.

Then, as you read in Part One, after Mom shared her boundaries with Travis, he let loose. We never had boundaries before, and he was not happy. He did everything in his power to hit her where it hurt. I didn't want the same for me. I no longer cared what he thought. My boundaries were tucked away in my journal for safe keeping.

Next followed all the things that happened with Karen and Travis wanting help then filing a motion saying we are liars with a vendetta. I was back to feeling like a crazy person. Now the boundaries I'd set didn't seem fulfilling to me. Back in September, the boundaries I set helped me forgive him. But after everything that happened, I didn't feel like forgiving him anymore. I just wanted him to own up to what he'd done instead of running from it and blaming everyone else. For the past year, I'd been racking my brain to understand why he just won't do that. I felt like, if I forgave him, it would excuse all the lies. I didn't want to dismiss the lies like nothing ever happened. I was lost again.

Then one day, I was scrolling through Facebook and one of my friends posted that they just finished the book *Boundaries* by Drs. Henry Cloud & John Townsend (2017). She said it was a game changer.

Since I was past the point of trying to find out what was wrong with Travis and was focusing on myself, I instantly bought the book. My friend was right, it was a game changer.

One thing that really stuck out to me was in the section about boundary conflicts in family. The book states, "An irresponsible adult child depends on a responsible adult sibling to avoid growing up and leaving the family. The irresponsible child continues to play old family games well into adulthood" (Cloud and Townsend 2017). Okay, that makes sense. I could see that dynamic playing out in my relationship with my brother.

I finished the book and had a better understanding of what boundaries are and why they are necessary. But I didn't actually *do* any work.

A few weeks later, after yet another "event" that left me spiraling with questions, Roxanne told me it was time to do the work. This work was looking at my flaws and seeing how they've played a role in this situation and how they've affected my boundaries. Of course, no one wants to look at their own flaws, but I was already starting to see success in the work she was having me do, so I opened the book again and really dug deep.

Within the chapter "Boundaries and Family" there is a section called "Resolution of Boundary Problems with Family." It states that "establishing boundaries with families of origin is a tough task but one with great reward. It is a process with certain distinguishable steps" (Cloud and Townsend 2017). The following steps are taken from that section:[5]

Step 1: Identify the symptom

"Where have you lost control of your property?"

When I was a teen, I didn't have any boundaries (do any teens?), so I just went with the flow and did what I was told.

When Travis found sobriety, I still didn't have control of my property. I allowed him to roam freely in my fenced yard because I was excited to have him sober. I was also excited that he was back in my life and we could have the relationship we'd had when we were kids. How could I shut out someone I love and care about? And I trusted him. I never in a million years thought he would destroy my property or abuse his access to all my things (metaphorically).

Then, when I found out he had started drinking again, I felt like I was wandering my property trying to find him, but he was not there. For the past ten years, he had always been right there — a phone call away. When he would show up drunk or angry, or call me, he would barge in my yard and throw stones at my house.

Because I had always let him roam free on my property, the minute I closed my gate, he took it as a direct attack on him, like he wasn't good enough for me. The reality is, I had to close the door because I had to protect myself from two things: seeing him under the influence, which brought back many painful memories from my childhood, and being his punching bag. All

---

5 The steps in this chapter are all taken from Boundaries (Cloud and Townsend 2017).

the consequences he was facing were due to his choices, choices *he* was making, not because of anything I did or didn't do.

I don't blame him for being angry. Because of our whole family's lack of boundaries, he suffered. He never really had to deal with his natural consequences because there was always someone who would pick him up, lie for him, and support him even when his choices were not in his best interest.

One would think that, when Travis got sober, the dynamic of the family protecting him would change. But it didn't. Even though he wasn't using substances, there were times when he would make poor choices in other areas of his life. Yet we wouldn't say anything. We still protected him from his natural consequences because we didn't want him to relapse.

My symptom — I had no boundaries.

Step 2: Identify the conflict

"What 'law boundaries' are you violating? See yourself as the problem and find your boundary violations."

My first thought when I read this exercise was, *Wait a minute. My brother is the one with the problem, why do I have to look at what I'm doing wrong? How could I possibly be doing anything wrong?*

This is a common thing we hear all the time from parents and siblings. *Why do I have to work on myself? I'm not the one with the substance use problem.* And even though I *know* that working on myself is important, I was reluctant. Still, I promised myself I would keep an open mind and maybe learn something about myself.

As I opened up to the chapter on the ten laws of boundaries, I quickly learned I wasn't as perfect as I thought I was. I was breaking five of the ten laws. Fifty percent of what I was doing was wrong! Of course, all of this contributed to my brother's addiction. Here are the five laws[6] in which I failed him and myself:

---

6 The laws in Step 2 are all taken from Boundaries (Cloud and Townsend 2017).

The Law of Sowing and Reaping

"Rescuing a person from the natural consequences of his behavior enables him to continue in irresponsible behavior."

For my whole life and my brother's, our parents lovingly rescued us from everything. If I forgot a homework assignment at home, my mom would rush it over to school. If I had money issues, my parents would bail me out. Every time Travis would get an underage drinking ticket, Mom would go to court and pay the fine. We were lucky and blessed to have parents who loved us so much.

But at the same time, this saving didn't do us any good. I'm not sure if our parents rescued us because it was something their parents did or didn't do for them in their childhood, but I don't think it was intentional; they just wanted us to be happy.

I don't feel that I violate this law often because I *do* let people suffer their natural consequences. But I hate to see people suffer, and I wish, at times, there were things I could do to help them, even at my own expense. It is a real struggle not to jump in and save them, even when I'm sick to my stomach thinking of them suffering.

I'm much more conscious of this now than ever before because of what I am going through with my brother's relapse. Even when he was sober, I believe I protected him from his consequences because I didn't want him to relapse. Now, for the first time ever in his life, he is dealing with his own consequences. It sucks to watch him lose everything, but I have to remember that *he* did this and *he* needs to deal with the consequences.

Learning this information was also an eye opener for me as a mom. Every morning I would ask my kids, "Do you have your Chromebook? Your homework? Is you snack packed? Are your teeth brushed? Is your hair combed? Are your shoes on?" Then one day, I said to myself, *Why am I doing this?* When they leave my house one day to venture out on their own, I'm not going to be there to make sure they have everything or have done what they need to have done. I am doing a disservice to my children. So I stopped. I taught them how to do their own laundry so they have clean clothes for school the next day. I talked to them about being prepared for school and, if they forget something, I will not bring it for them. I would much rather them learn the hard way now, then flounder through life as an adult because I did everything for them as a child.

The Law of Power

"You cannot change others. More people suffer from trying to change others than from any other sickness. What you can do is influence them. Since you cannot get them to change, you must change yourself so that their destructive patterns no longer work on you."

When someone we love is addicted to substances, we want them to change. We know that if they give up the substance, their lives will be better. But they don't see it that way. Most of the time, that substance is the only thing that makes them feel better — temporarily.

Our natural tendency is to tell them what they need to do to change, but that is what keeps *us* sick. We are so fixated on changing them, we lose sight of ourselves.

And this is absolutely what happened to me when Travis relapsed. I love him so much, and I wanted him to change back to the old fun-loving, sober person he used to be. It consumed me, my thoughts, my time, and my energy. Yes, it was coming from a place of love and compassion, but he didn't change. And I stayed sick.

This is one of the areas that I've been focusing a lot of energy on. How can I take that need for wanting him to change and redirect all that energy to bettering myself? It hasn't been easy and has taken some time.

When you live in this place for so many years, it's hard to break the habits. The first thing I learned to do when I thought about Travis was to redirect my thoughts. For example, I would think to myself, *Why is he acting like this? All of this is happening because he's drinking. Why can't he see this?* Then I would take a moment to redirect my thoughts because I knew if I didn't, I would spend hours internally looping these questions that would never get answered. So I would acknowledge the questions then remind myself that it is out of my control and try to focus on what I was going to do that day for myself or with my kids. Every time he would start taking up room in my thoughts, I would acknowledge it and redirect my thoughts to something else.

After some time of practicing this, I started to have fewer and fewer thoughts of him to the point where they rarely ever cross my mind.

If I hadn't taken this step and really, truly convinced myself that I cannot change him, I would still be in the vicious cycle.

After doing this exercise, I wrote myself a goal. My goal was to continue to grow myself which would hopefully help influence others to grow as well. This lesson really helped me forgive Travis and find my voice, both of which I will talk about in later chapters.

The Law of Motivation

"Freedom first, service second. If your giving is not leading to cheer, then you need to examine the law of motivation."

The law of motivation tells us that, because we are loving people, we are afraid to set boundaries because if we say no, people might love us less or abandon us. They might get angry at us. Or we'll be lonely.

When Travis got sober, I was afraid to set boundaries with him because I was afraid that I would lose him.

You'll hear this theme over and over, but I thought if I told him no, he would relapse. Or he'd get angry at me. Travis's anger is scary, and I did not want to poke the bear. It was much easier to say yes to him than to deal with his wrath.

So every time something was bothering him and he asked me to meet him, I'd drop everything I was doing and meet with him for a couple hours and try to help him feel better. But that didn't help anyone. It got to a point where I was giving so much of my time that my giving was *not* leading me to cheer.

After he relapsed (it had been a couple of months), he had asked me to meet and I said no. I told him I didn't have time to get up and leave my family, but he was more than welcome to call me that night to talk over the phone. He was livid and didn't understand. I told him that I've dropped everything for him to listen to his struggles, and they've all been a lie (not once did he ever tell me he had been drinking). I said I was no longer going to meet him, that he could talk to me over the phone, and he has never called since.

He had already relapsed so that fear was gone. Was he angry at me for not meeting with him? Hell yes. But I survived his anger. I had to remind myself of the previous law: "You must change yourself so that their destructive patterns no longer work on you."

This law violation has carried over into other aspects of my life. I know for a fact that I'm afraid to say no to people because I'm afraid they won't like me or I'll hurt their feelings. I usually put everyone else before my own needs, and I get burned out.

I watch other people say no with such ease and I'm jealous. Why can't it be that easy for me?

But now that I have learned this about myself, I'm working on saying no and not overextending myself to the point where I have nothing left for me. And guess what? No one hates me, and I haven't hurt anyone's feelings, yet. I feel much better about myself because I am making time for myself.

After completing this exercise, I set a boundary with *myself*: If it doesn't fit in my schedule, I don't do it.

The Law of Proactivity

"You need to practice and gain assertiveness. You need to get far enough away from abusive people to be able to fence your property against further invasion. And then you need to own the treasures you find in your soul."

I have been, and still am at times, a passive and compliant person which can lead to me being reactive.

I think that this stems back to my younger years when Travis first began using substances. If I would speak up about how I felt about Travis's use and what my parents were doing about it, I would get shut down, or no one would listen to me. Being passive and compliant as a teen was a way for me to avoid making things worse at home.

While it may have protected me in my younger years, it does me no good now as an adult. As the book says, "Those who are passive and compliant build up rage and then they react by going ballistic" (Cloud and Townsend 2017).

This reactive stage does not serve a positive purpose. While it's good to get everything out, I tend to say things I regret or in a way that doesn't bring to light my true feelings.

Let me give you an example.

In February 2020, after not talking to Travis since October, we finally sat down as a family. We let him start the conversation, and all he wanted to focus on was why I told Cindy about his drinking. He didn't want to talk about what happened when he drove the dump truck drunk or anything he had done in the past four months. It was all focused on everything *we* had done wrong. After five minutes of him telling us how horrible we were for telling Cindy about his relapse, we were done and said we were not going to discuss it anymore. We told him, "End of story; move on." He got up and walked out. That's when I'd yelled, "Don't be a coward and come back and talk to us!"

Maybe that was not the best thing to say in the situation, but I had so much pent up hurt. I felt like he was being a coward, which he was, but yelling that to him probably wasn't the best idea. All we wanted from the conversation was for him to be open and honest about his drinking, and he wasn't ready for that at that point.

When I link this back to setting boundaries, it was like I let him on my property, he yelled and screamed nasty things to me and about me, and I took it. Then I snapped and kicked him off my property. Without boundaries, we allow people to walk all over us until we can't take it anymore. And when we snap, *we* look like the crazy ones.

Boundaries allow you to be proactive versus reactive. "While reactive victims are primarily known by their 'against' stances, proactive people do not demand rights, they live them" (Cloud and Townsend 2017).

Looking back at the situation with Travis from that February and in other instances of my life, I can absolutely see how being reactive took away my power in the situation. Being reactive is normal, but controlling the reactivity is where the power lies. Travis did return to the conversation ten minutes later, but he had a smirk on his face the whole time because he got a reaction out of me. I lost my cool, and now he held the power.

With the work I've done on myself over the past couple of years, I can see the growth in this area. For one, I have become more assertive. Keeping things bottled up causes me to lose it at some point and hurt the people I love. Addressing things as they happen has changed my life.

I've also had a significant amount of time away from Travis. When he first relapsed and probably even for the first year afterwards, I was unable to see the manipulation. To be honest, I probably didn't want to believe that my brother, who meant the world to me, was even capable of that level of manipulation. Yes, I was in denial.

But since I have had the time to heal, I can see it clear as day. I've had the time to build my fence so that history doesn't repeat itself.

If I could redo the entire conversation I had with Travis in February, I would have waited longer than four months, given myself more time to heal, and had professionals there to help.

The Law of Exposure

"We secretly resent instead of telling someone that we are angry about how they have hurt us. Often, we will privately endure the pain of someone's irresponsibility instead of telling them how their behavior affects us, information that would be helpful to their soul."

I think this law violation ties back to me being a passive person afraid to lose a friendship or hurt someone. It is easier to just let things slide than to address them head on. I have this fear that, if I tell someone how I feel, they will leave me or get so angry at me that they never talk to me again. This fear has kept me paralyzed.

When I look back at Travis's relapse, this law violation really hurt my brother. Not only did I violate this law by not telling Travis about how his behavior affected me, but my parents never told him either. In the book it states, "Parents will 'love' their children by giving in over and over for years, not setting limits, and resenting the love they are showing. The children grow up never feeling loved because of the lack of honesty, and their parents are befuddled, thinking, *after all we've done..."* (Cloud and Townsend 2017). This is exactly what happened with my parents. By violating this law, they, too, hurt him by loving him too much.

When Travis was sober, I wish I would have told him how his behavior affected me. There were times he would get so angry when we were stuck in traffic coming home from a presentation that he would snap at me like it was my fault. It obviously wasn't my fault, but he took it out on me. Did I do or say anything to defend myself or verbalize my feelings? No. My friend later told me that she couldn't believe I had said nothing to him. Remember, though, I was afraid to say anything.

Another example is when we went on a trip to Colorado. Members of our "Stairway to Heroin" team were selected to go to Colorado and present at a national conference. So Katie, my co-worker and friend, and Travis and his wife, and I decided to tag along. We thought of it as a work retreat. While the team was presenting at the conference, Katie, Travis, Karen, and I went hiking. When we got back, we all had to take a quick shower and get dressed because everyone was meeting up at 5:30 for our dinner reservation. At 5:35, Travis and Karen were not in the lobby. Worried that we would miss our dinner reservation, we called to find out where they were. They said they needed more time but not in a nice way. Our group was waiting for them, and Travis yelled in the phone so loudly that everyone nearby could hear him on my cell phone. Of course, Mom and I let it slide because we were used to him being this way.

The next night, Katie, Mom, another one of our friends, and I had dinner together. Both of our friends, very nicely, asked Mom and me why we allowed Travis to speak to us that way. It was really the first "oh shit" moment for us. We were so used to it, we were blind to the fact he was completely disrespectful.

All through his ten years, or however long he was truly sober, we allowed him to be rude, cocky, arrogant, and disrespectful, chalking it up to "that's just how he is."

If we would have said something to him when he was out of line, it would have been good for his soul. Even though I know the consequences he faces are due to his choices, I can't help but think that maybe if I would have told him how he made us feel, maybe, just maybe, he wouldn't have relapsed. Not putting him in his place fueled his ego, making him think he could and do anything he wanted to.

Now that we aren't afraid to call him out, he has shut us out of his life. It was our biggest fear, but it has also been our biggest blessing. He will continue until he seeks help.

My goal for all my relationships going forward is to recognize when I want to let things slide and speak my feelings when it's beneficial for myself and the other person.

Step 3: Identify the need that drives the conflict

After reading Part One, it's probably obvious that my underlying needs are to be protected, heard, and accepted.

Growing up in the environment I did, I never felt like anyone was in my corner protecting me. I had to grow up fast which meant protecting myself. I had no voice and didn't feel like anyone really accepted me.

Reflecting back, I feel like maybe I was looking for that from my brother once he got sober. He would protect me, listen to me, and accept who I was. But I don't think I ever got that from him because everything was always about him. I lived in his shadow even when he was sober.

In my adult life, I want to protect others. I don't like seeing people hurting. But this *need* to protect others comes at a cost — not sticking to my boundaries and me ultimately getting hurt.

It may have taken me over twenty-six years, but I finally found my voice — more about this in a later chapter.

As far as feeling accepted, that's still a work in progress.

Step 4: Take in and receive the good

"Do not continue to hide yourself in the ground and expect to get better. Learn to respond to and receive love."

Asking for help when I am struggling is not an easy task for me. There were so many times when Travis was using substances that I felt I didn't have any support. So what was the point in even asking?

But that only hurt me in the long run.

After working with my counselor, I know how important support is. I've also learned that, if I ask for support and don't receive it, I'm not going to die; my life won't be over.

The more I have let go of Travis, the more my other relationships have grown, and the more support I have.

I didn't know how much support I really had until much later in my journey of healing.

Step 5: Practice boundary skills

Take baby steps, practicing saying *no* in safe and supported relationships. It's not easy, but the more you do it, the easier it gets.

Step 6: Say no to the bad.

"Avoid harmful situations, people who have abused you. Be careful not to get sucked into a controlling situation again because your wish for reconciliation is so strong."

When we are living in the world of a loved one's addiction, it's hard to not get sucked back into the drama and craziness.

When something happens, we're mad, angry, and upset, then we feel bad for them because we know addiction has such a strong and crazy pull. Then we think, *Maybe this was a one-time thing,* or, *I should be easy on them because I want things to get better or go back to how it used to be.* But when we do that — let things slide — we lose our boundaries.

In the early years, it was easy to get sucked back into the cycle because I didn't know any better.

Since I didn't learn any effective coping skills during my younger years when Travis had his period of recovery, as you have read, I let things fly. It was much easier to reconcile than to deal with his wrath.

After the relapse, a counselor friend said, "Don't rescue Travis. Don't jump into trying to help or fix him; let him figure it out himself." And even though that was hard because we sincerely wanted to help him, and we didn't quite fully understand *how* it would work or *if* it would work, we heeded his advice and let Travis go.

Don't get me wrong, there were times when we thought, *Let's just have a family meeting and move on. Then everything will go back to normal, like nothing ever happened.*

But even if Travis was willing to meet, it would not have worked. None of us were healthy enough to hold our boundaries. We all would have slipped back into the cycle of his addiction that we had been riding for so long.

Now, there have been times over the past two years when Travis reached out to either Mom or Dad and acted like nothing ever happened. It would have been easy for them to fall into old patterns, forget about what happened, and move on. But my parents didn't do that. They held true to their own personal boundaries. As you can imagine, Travis did not like it one bit.

I kind of think of this step like a kid who doesn't get their way and has a temper tantrum. Let's say your child cries hysterically every time you take away their iPad. After five minutes of the screaming, you can no longer take it, so you hand the iPad back to your child and say, "You can have five more minutes if you stop crying." But then you take it away and the cycle starts all over again. If you would have stuck to your guns the first time, the child would've learned that when you say they are done, you mean it.

For too many years, we unknowingly allowed this behavior from Travis. He would do something inappropriate, rude, etc., and we would just *let it slide* because *he was in recovery*. So when we finally put our foot down, he had temper tantrum after temper tantrum and would not give in.

After doing this piece of the boundary work, I wrote a new boundary for myself: I will not have contact with Travis or Karen until I am strong enough and their words no longer hurt. I have stuck with this boundary since the day I wrote it.

This was the first time in my journey when I took a step back and said, *I need to work more on myself.* Up until this point, I was just going through the motions like a checklist. This is done, that is done, I should feel better, right? But this piece made me realize that boundary setting isn't going to magically take away the pain, hurt, anger, and sadness. We all want a quick fix, but this work is not quick. We actually have to put in time and conscious effort. While we are setting our boundaries, we also need to work on addressing those feelings.

Step 7: Forgive the aggressor

"When you refuse to forgive someone, you still want something from that person, and even if it is revenge that you want, it keeps you tied to that person forever."

Huh? Come again? Did I read that right? I have to forgive him? The pain is so deep, how the hell am I supposed to forgive him? If I forgive him, does that mean that everything he's done is okay?

After reading this short section a hundred times, I gritted my teeth and wrote very firmly with my pen:

Travis, I forgive you for breaking my trust, for saying untrue things about me to others, and for lying to the court.

There, I did it. Why don't I feel better?

It wasn't until later on, when I was truly ready, that I did the work on forgiveness. This will be addressed in the next chapter because this work is HARD.

Step 8: Respond, don't react

"If someone is able to cause havoc by doing or saying something, she is in control of you at that point, and your boundaries are lost. When you respond, you remain in control with options and choices."

This has seriously been another hard step for me. It seemed like everything that had happened was so far-fetched that it was hard not to react.

At the time I did this exercise, I literally found out that day that Travis told the judge and the guardian ad litem that he only drank one time and immediately checked himself into IOP.

Travis claimed that he never drank before that, and we, my parents and I, fabricated the story because he wanted to leave the family and we didn't want him to leave. This could not be further from the truth. But, according to the guardian ad litem, his two therapists and his sponsor believed this to be true. It was hard not to react because his claims were so *crazy* and a flat-out lie! I wish to God he only drank once and checked into IOP; our story would be a lot different.

But I have to remember what the book says. When we react, *they* are in control (Cloud and Townsend 2017). And that is what Travis loves the most. When we *respond*, *we* are in control.

How do we respond without reacting? It took me some time to figure out the difference. The first thing to do is take some deep breaths. Our initial reaction is exactly that, our *reaction*. When I heard that Travis lied in front of the judge, my reaction was to call or text him and tell him my thoughts. But that would have given him power. He would have loved to have known that his actions hurt me.

After stewing about it for a little bit, I found my response: *He can say whatever he wants, but we (Travis, Karen, Cindy, Mom, Dad, his sponsor, and I) all know the truth.* I never shared that with him, but that is how I kept myself from going crazy. That was the response I would tell myself every time something would happen. And it gave me peace. Am I pissed that he lies? *Yes*, but there is nothing I can do about it. Nothing I say or do will stop him. I have to do what's best for me and remember that we all know the truth.

Step 9: Learn to love in freedom and responsibility, not in guilt

"Boundaries in no way mean to stop loving. They mean the opposite: you are gaining the freedom to love."

This last part really reinforces for me how important it is to have boundaries in place. When we sacrifice our time, money, and energy out of guilt, we are the ones who lose. When we give because we want to, we have true freedom.

In the past, before I worked on healing myself, I spent too much of my time giving into Travis's wants and needs because I was afraid I would feel guilty. I was afraid that if I did or said the wrong thing, or didn't do enough for him, something would happen to him. I was afraid that my own actions weren't enough to keep him sober (even though that was *not* my job). I always felt like whatever I did was never enough for him. Most of all, I was afraid that if something were to happen, I would live with that guilt the rest of my life. And I felt bad for him, pitied him. Here he was — a single father, a new father, a lost soul, newly married ... fill in the blank. The combination of fear of guilt and pity, blinded me from what was really going on.

Now that I no longer feel the guilt, I can give purposely, and it feels good!

Whew! That was a lot of hard work but well worth it. I learned so much from the work I did on myself that it really helped me grow.

Looking back at my September boundaries for Travis, they are pretty much the same now as far as what I will and will not do. The fence, for now, is a brick wall all the way around my property with no gate. I will not let Travis or Karen step foot on my property until my grass is green and my flowers are in bloom. I will love from a distance.

Although I started this boundary work with the goal to set boundaries with my brother, I applied this work to all my relationships and the people in my life.

The boundaries I have set for myself are:

• I only say "yes" to things that are important to me and fit into my schedule.

• If I feel like someone is out of line, I will tell them if it's good for their soul and mine.

• I will speak my mind.

• I will stay true and authentic to myself.

My advice: Go by the book and do the work! You will not regret it!

Forgiveness

"Forgive others, not because they deserve
forgiveness, but because you deserve peace."
–— Mel Robbins

When I first started doing boundary work, forgiveness was hard. In the book *Boundaries*, which I spoke about in the previous chapter, it says that, if we don't forgive, we can't move on from what happened (Cloud and Townsend 2017).

I had forgiven Travis for what he did when he was a teenager. At presentations, people would often ask how I was able to forgive him after everything he had put us through. I would always reply that I was able to separate Travis-my-brother from Travis-who-used-drugs. When Travis was getting the help he needed, he took responsibility for the things he did and worked every day to be the great person he was, and it was easy to forgive him. As my relationship with Travis-my-brother strengthened, the things that Travis-who-used-drugs did started to fade away. Eventually it got to the point where it no longer mattered what happened in the past because my relationship with Travis-my-brother was so strong. I had forgiven him.

When he relapsed after several years of sobriety, it was actually easy to forgive his alcohol usage after I had time to process it. What I had a hard time forgiving was the lying. How could I possibly forgive someone who was lying about what happened? The struggle for me was harder this time because it was the opposite of what had happened in the past. In the past, Travis owned up to what he was doing. This time he refused. I could forgive Travis-who-used-drugs, but I couldn't forgive Travis-my-brother for the betrayal.

That was, until I read that forgiveness and reconciliation are two different things. We forgive people for *us*; it allows us to move on. Reconciliation is when two people come together to own up to their part and take responsibility for their own actions. We can forgive people but never reconcile. The *Boundaries* book states, "Do not think that because you have forgiven that you have to reconcile. You can offer reconciliation, but it must be contingent on the other person owning her behavior and bringing forth trustworthy fruits" (Cloud and Townsend 2017).

Once I read that section, it made total sense to me. I was afraid to forgive him because I didn't want him to think that the lying and deceit was ok. I wanted him to own up to what he did. Period. But this understanding that I can forgive and move on with my life without giving him a pass on his behavior was a game changer for me. But, just like everything else, it took time. Yes, I could say I had forgiven him, but deep down inside I hadn't fully yet.

Gabrielle Bernstein explains in her book, *The Universe Has Your Back*, that by not forgiving someone, you make yourself the victim. Another interesting concept. To be honest, when I first read that, I thought, *I'm not playing the victim!* My defenses were real.

Then, after some time, I had an "ah-ha" moment, *Maybe I am playing the victim*. I felt that, because he hurt me with the lies, he owes me. By holding onto the feeling that he owes me, I was unable to forgive. Then I realized that I'm *not* the victim. He owes me nothing. In fact, I want nothing from him.

As I look back at the situation and the events that happened, I am thankful for how things played out. He didn't get help right away which allowed his true colors to show. If he would have gotten help right away, things would have gone back to the way they were. And by the way they were, I mean us putting Travis on a pedestal, worrying about what he said, tiptoeing on eggshells because of his anger, and worrying about his sobriety. I would have remained living in the shadows. I would never have experienced the life I have now, the pure happiness I feel in every part of my being.

I don't feel the hurt, betrayal, or anger anymore. Having forgiving him, I feel free. He has given me a gift greater than anything, even greater than his sobriety. *I am no victim.*

I know siblings that have lost their loved ones, and, even though they are sad that they died and miss them terribly, there is a sense of relief that it's over, that they no longer have to worry. Although mine is still living, by forgiving him — all of him — I have a sense of relief that it's over. Sure, I could get the call one day that he passed away, but I would tell people that he gave me the greatest gift of freedom. I have made peace with what has happened and who he is, but that was only realized by forgiving him.

I no longer hope for his sobriety. His sobriety doesn't make him who he is. My hope for him is that he can find the peace and happiness he has given me, whether he is sober or not.

I'm sure, if he was writing this, he would say he could never forgive me for what I did, for telling the mother of his firstborn that he was drinking again. I hope, for his sake — not mine, that he can forgive me so that he can move on.

This step of forgiveness was the hardest of all steps. It took me two years of hard work to complete this, but it has been the most rewarding step of all.

There are moments when things happen where I want to be angry with him, and I feel like I need an explanation from him to make sense of everything. When that happens, I have to remind myself that I don't need answers from him. I know the truth; I can live with each and every decision I have made. At the end of the day, he has to live with the decisions he has made.

Forgiveness is not one and done. At least for me, it's something that I am continuously working on. I feel like, when I forgive one thing, something else happens. First I forgave the drinking. Then I forgave the lying. Now I'm working on forgiving other things that have been brought to my attention since I've removed myself from his life.

Let me give you an example. I was in such a great place with my healing with Travis. I had forgiven him, and I was feeling indifferent towards him. Then a good friend of mine told me that, three years prior, she had received a text from him asking if she would have sex with him if he paid her. At this time, Travis was married and expecting his first child with Karen, and my friend was married with children. This was such a shock to me. I'd suspected that he'd had relationships outside of his marriage, but to ask my close friend? *That* I could not understand. I was also surprised she never told me. She said she felt she handled it well and there was no need to bring it up. But I felt bad that she had been carrying this for the last three years.

If I'm 100% honest, if she would have told me three years prior, I would have minimized it. I probably would have chalked it up to him having another fight with his wife and looking for an escape. However, that day I felt another betrayal by him. I thought I knew him. I never in a million years thought he would approach my friends like that. Now it makes me wonder if he tried to solicit anyone else I know for sex, or what other things he did while we all thought he was in a good place. So I had to work on forgiving *this* side of him, which was tough, because I felt like our whole ten-year relationship was a lie; I was a sucker in his game.

I share this, not to throw him under the bus, but to show that even once we have forgiven someone, things can happen that can make us question our forgiveness. We might have to do the work again to forgive this new thing. But once we practice forgiveness, it does get easier to forgive again. I spent one whole weekend pissed at Travis for soliciting my friend. Then I remembered that being pissed holds me to him, and forgiving sets me free. I forgave him for what he did, though that does not make what he did ok. I reminded myself that *he* has to live with the choices he made.

If you are struggling like I was to forgive a loved one, I encourage you to hang in there. Keep trying. The longer you hold on to them, the less time and energy you have for yourself. Forgive and move on with *your* life.

Hitting Rock Bottom

> "Just when you think you've hit rock bottom,
> someone will hand you a shovel."
> — Jill Shalvis

We hear the term "rock bottom" over and over again when talking about addiction. What does that really mean? Is everyone's rock bottom the same? How do you know if someone has hit their rock bottom?

In Travis's early addiction, there were many times when we thought he was at his rock bottom. Every time he got arrested, or when his unborn son passed away, my parents and I were like, *This is it, he's going to finally get help this time.* But he never did.

My mom used to say that she forced that rock bottom for Travis when they kicked him out of the house for good. Looking back now, it still wasn't his rock bottom — she didn't force it. It was actually *her* rock bottom; she couldn't take any more and *her* rock bottom forced him to change.

About a year into Travis's relapse, my co-worker and friend, Katie, and I did a podcast with our friend AJ. AJ is a clinical supervisor and counselor who's been working in the field of substance abuse for over sixteen years. He also hosts his own podcast, *Talking Addiction & Recovery*. We invited him to guest speak on our podcast, *Prevent This!,* about some of the challenges of treatment. He told us that oftentimes parents or loved ones will catch their loved one in the act, let's say drinking alcohol, and feel relieved, like, *See? I caught you. Time to give it up.* But more times than not, it doesn't change anything.

That conversation really resonated with me. When Travis relapsed and I found out about it, I felt like, *Everyone knows now; he'll change his ways.* Unfortunately, that didn't happen. He continued drinking.

Months later, after he stopped talking to me, I kind of pushed it to the side, no longer worrying about what was going to be his rock bottom to make him get help. I prayed every night that he was doing better.

Then, as time went on, I would hear things, or he wouldn't show up for his son's football practice, and my gut would scream, *He's starting the cycle again!* Although I couldn't prove it, I just knew. Then, two weeks later, his wife called and said he was missing. Again, my parents and I would think, *Ok, this is it, now he'll get help.* Again, he did not.

I hate to admit it, but there were times I wanted to catch him in the act. I would drive by a bar that I thought maybe he would frequent. I would drive by his house to see if he was home. I wanted to catch him just to say, *See? I know you're still drinking. Please, let's get some help.*

But we never caught him in the act. He did call our mom drunk a handful of times. But, so far, he's been too smart to get caught. All communication has been through phone calls or very vague texts. He would never put anything in writing to implicate himself.

I can't describe the feeling of when my gut is screaming *something is wrong* and my mind is worried, and I just want proof so I don't feel like I'm going crazy. I can imagine the feeling is the same if you felt that your spouse was cheating on you (and that's why people hire private investigators). Every time my gut screamed, I'd find out three to four weeks later why.

To be honest, it was making me sick. I thought to myself, *Why am I putting in so much effort when he's putting in zero effort to prove he's sober? Why am I worrying myself sick?* If I were truly an important person in his life and he was healthy, he would at least say, "I'm doing well, thanks."

And since my efforts provided zero evidence, I gave up. My mom always tells families that the burden of proof that they are sober is on them. It's not your job to prove they are using.

Bottom line: catching them does not mean they will see the need for help. For some it might, for others the denial becomes stronger. In my situation, every time he slipped up and got caught, there was no proof. With no proof, he would deny it, people would believe him, and that empowered him to continue doing what he was doing.

What this lesson taught me is that we can get stuck in the cycle of waiting for them to hit rock bottom so that they will change. But no one knows what their rock bottom will be. Or they could hit rock bottom a hundred times and still not change. And we lose more hope with each cycle.

But what I've realized in my journey is that we can't wait for them to hit rock bottom because that is uncertain. What is more important is for *us* to find *our* rock bottom. How much are we going to tolerate? How much will we let this dictate our lives? Do we want to live everyday questioning if today will be the day that they get help? At what point will we say enough is enough? Boundary work is what helps us decide what our rock bottom is. It gives us the power back to take control of our lives.

If you're in a situation where you just want proof, stop looking. Have faith that it will present itself. Searching for proof can make you sick, taking away time from your loved ones and yourself. Find *your* rock bottom and let go.

Other Shadow Children

"Most people carry that pain around inside them their whole lives, until they kill the pain by other means, or until it kills them. But you, my friends, you found another way: a way to use the pain. To burn it as fuel, for light and warmth. You have learned to break the world that has tried to break you."

— Lev Grossman

Over the years I have met several people who have very similar stories to mine. Their siblings got caught up in substance use.

About ten years ago, my mom and I attended a presentation about opiate use at a local high school. This was right before the opioid crisis devastated our country. There were two presenters, Frank and Chris, and they both worked for the local metro drug unit. During the presentation, Chris would refer to users as junkies, addicts with no life or purpose, homewreckers, and some other not-so-nice words.

After the presentation, my mom walked right up to Chris — mind you Chris is a 300 pound, burley, no BS detective — and said, "These junkies are someone's child, and I don't appreciate you talking about them like that."

Surprisingly, he took her feedback quite well, and we quickly became friends.

We started speaking together about substances — him from the law enforcement perspective and us from the family perspective — at local high schools. He ended up joining the Your Choice board of directors.

About four years into our friendship, at one of our "Stairway to Heroin" presentations, Chris took the stage and said, "I'm a cop, past president of the Wisconsin Narcotics Officers Association, and my brother is a heroin addict."

That statement hit me like a ton of bricks. It took me back to when we first met him. I immediately understood the frustration, anger, and sadness he felt when he talked about those who abuse opioids. For years, Chris had been fighting the war on drugs on the streets, but the battle was still going on at home. I felt an instant connection to him. We were fighting the same battle, but my brother had found sobriety, and his brother had not yet.

Chris often shared with us that seeing Travis sober gave him hope that one day his brother would find the same sobriety. Over the years, his brother did have periods of sobriety.

When Travis relapsed, Chris took it just as hard as we did. At that moment, he lost all hope for his brother. But he never gave up on him.

Unfortunately, when Chris's brother didn't answer the phone one day, Chris went to his house and found him. He had overdosed and passed away.

On the car ride to the funeral with my mom, I was brutally honest with her. I said, "Is it awful of me to feel jealous of Chris?" I wasn't jealous because his brother died, and I don't wish death on my brother, but I envied that it was over for Chris. He no longer had to worry what his brother was doing or if he was sober, or clean up the messes his brother made, or have to deal with his parents' guilt and shame. Chris had closure, something that I didn't yet have.

Back when Travis was using in his younger years, I would secretly ask God to take him if this was how the rest of our lives were going to be because it was too hard to live this way. Even as recently as his relapse, there were times I cried on the bathroom floor wishing for it to be over.

I have another friend, Dee, who has also lived a very similar journey to mine. Her brother was charismatic, outgoing, and everyone loved him. He was also addicted to substances and was an excellent manipulator. All very similar traits as my brother.

She and I can tell stories of our brothers, and the stories are eerily similar. We also can laugh and cry together, reminiscing about all we've been through on this journey.

Unfortunately, like Chris, her brother also passed away from an overdose. During one of our conversations, she confessed that she was glad it was over (*not* that her brother had died — she misses him dearly) because it was a closure for her, an ending. She could move on with her life.

Again, I felt jealous. There I was, still floundering without closure, still living this cycle of Travis's addiction. As hard as I tried to get away from it, I couldn't. Yet, at the same time, I was mad at myself for feeling that way. *How could somebody want their sibling to die? I must be an awful person.* For the longest time, I teetered between wanting him to die and being hopeful that my brother would be sober again. I could never find the right words to explain this paradox. That is, until I learned about "ambiguous loss."

During a recent conversation with Dee, she said, "You need to learn to be indifferent about the situation with your brother. If you feel hate, which I do at times, then you are tying an emotion to him. And having that tie to him will keep you sick. If you can get to a place of indifference, then you have truly let go."

This advice came at such a perfect time. Football season was starting, and I would undoubtedly run into Travis at least once a week. Now I'm in such a good place that I can see him and not shake, my heart doesn't start pumping, and I don't want to run. When I see him, I feel like he is one of the player's parents that I have never met. I feel *indifferent*. Dee's right, it is a great place to be.

How did I get to this place of indifference? I set my boundaries, I forgave all that he has done, I learned about ambiguous loss, and I allowed myself to grieve the loss of the brother that I knew (more to come on this).

These two amazing friends of mine have dedicated their lives to helping others, using their pain to do something great. Chris is a detective and has spent many years getting drugs off the street. Dee became a counselor, opened up a counseling center, and helps people struggling with mental health.

I have also run groups at local high schools for siblings of substance abusers. I can tell you, the stories are similar as well as the pain. But having friends who genuinely understand, listen to me, and can give some advice is very healing. No one wants to feel alone or like no one understands them. In my teen years, I shut it out. I pretended that it wasn't happening so that I didn't feel alone. The fact that society is more open now to addressing these issues is a game changer.

Most of my friends have lost their siblings. I also have friends whose siblings are in recovery, but they don't talk about the past. It's like they closed that chapter of their life with a lock and threw away the key. They don't ever, ever want to talk about what happened. And that's totally okay.

One night after a presentation, a lady in her sixties came up to me. She said her story was similar to mine and she had been in therapy for the last twenty years, but what I'd said on stage had hit her like a ton of bricks. She had never been able to verbalize or even make sense of her feelings, but, in ten minutes, I had put words to her feelings, and she was so grateful.

Some say that God puts people in your path for a reason. These people have been placed in my path for a reason. They remind me that I'm not alone, the feelings I feel are normal, and the experiences I have lived through can make me stronger. They have proven to me that, even through the pain, we *can* continue to help others.

My advice is to look at the people that have been placed in your path. They are there to comfort you, challenge you, and even to help you see things a different way. If you are feeling alone, like no one in your life understands you, I recommend seeking out connections. There are Facebook groups for siblings, Alateen, Alanon, and many other groups. Remember, YOU ARE NOT ALONE!

Ambiguous Loss

> "Ambiguous loss — the incomplete or uncertain loss."
> — Pauline Boss

One day at work, Katie brought in a book she was reading called *Hit Hard: One Family's Journey of Letting Go of What Was — And Learning to Live Well with What Is* by Pat McLeod, Tammy McLeod, and Cynthia Ruchti (2019). She told my mom and me that we had to read this book because it was exactly what we were going through.

The book is about a family whose son had a traumatic brain injury from playing football at the age of seventeen. Although he survived multiple brain surgeries, he was never the same mentally. The dad was happy that his son was alive and celebrated each milestone. The mom grieved the loss of what her son was and could have become. Since their grief was so different, it was hard for each of them to understand why the other parent acted the way they did, until they learned about ambiguous loss.

When talking about what I've been through, I often call it a living hell. My brother is still here physically, but he's not the same person. My envy of those who have lost their loved one was due to the closure they had. I had no closure. Everything in the future was unknown.

Learning about ambiguous loss and putting a name to what I and my parents have been feeling was such a huge relief. As was knowing that we were not alone in our experiences.

It also helped me better understand how each one of us — Mom, Dad, and I — were coping with this loss. Mom cried because she missed the relationship she had with Travis and what she could see for them in the future. My dad was on the opposite side of the spectrum. The son that he had was gone. Period. Me, I am somewhere in between. There are days when I miss him and the future I envisioned. Other days, he's gone and never coming back.

I remember Roxanne saying to my mom and me early on in the counseling sessions, "You have to stop hoping that he will get better because, truth be told, he may never come back. You have to live your lives." We spent so much time hoping he was getting the help he needed and thinking of ways that we could help him, that we became paralyzed in our own lives. At the time, I didn't want to believe that the old Travis would never come back, but she was right. I was putting my life on hold.

After reading *Hit Hard* (McLeod, McLeod, and Ruchti 2019) and having such an "ah-ha" moment, I decided to dig deeper into what ambiguous loss was, what it meant, and what I could do about it. I bought the book *Ambiguous Loss: Learning to Live with Unresolved Grief* by Pauline Boss (2000).

Pauline says that "of all the losses experienced in personal relationships, ambiguous loss is the most devastating because it remains unclear, indeterminate" (Boss 2000). "People with ambiguous loss feel helpless, anxious, depressed, and have conflicts within their relationships. This happens because:

A. we don't know if the loss is temporary or final

B. the uncertainty prevents people from adjusting to the ambiguity of their loss by reorganizing the roles and rules of their relationship with the loved one, so that the couple or family relationships freezes in place. If the person has not been shut out already, they hang on to the hope that things will return to the way they used to be.

C People are denied the symbolic rituals that ordinarily support a clear loss."

For my parents and me, we have no closure, no defining days when things started and ended. When we first started this journey with Travis's relapse, we were frozen, hoping and praying that it was just temporary. When it started to become apparent that things were not getting better, Dad shut Travis out, and Mom hung onto hope for a while. Now we are in the process of shutting out. Not because we don't love him anymore, but because we can't ride this rollercoaster any longer.

We also cannot accurately explain our loss to others. He didn't die. His Facebook page shows him as "doing well." Whether he is or not, we experienced a loss, a loss that many don't understand, a loss that has no support or understanding from the outside world.

This loss also ripples through families. I see it in my own children. Although I have explained to them, in kid terms, what happened and why Uncle T is no longer coming around, I don't think they could verbalize what they feel. While I'm no expert, I would guess they are also feeling a loss but don't quite understand why. Why doesn't he ever call them on holidays or their birthday? Why isn't he at events?

Pauline also explains ambiguous loss as a trauma that "goes on and on in what families describe as a roller-coaster ride, during which they alternate between hope and hopelessness" (Boss 2000). This had been our journey for the past two years. Travis or Karen would reach out for help, and we would have renewed hope. Then they said we were liars and that nothing we said was true, and we felt hopeless.

After learning more about ambiguous loss, I have learned there are two options: you can either choose to live in this "frozen grief" (and I've seen many people do it) for the rest of your life, or you can recognize the loss and move on.

And that's exactly what we have chosen to do, move on. Do we still have hope that he will one day get sober and have a relationship with the family? Absolutely. Do we still feel a tremendous loss? Hell, yes. But we no longer live in that space. When we feel sad, we grieve and move on. When we feel hopeless, we accept that and move on. But I want to stress that it has taken two years to get to this point. If I would have read this book right after the relapse, I would have said I wasn't ready to move on, that there was still hope. So if you are struggling right now, it's okay. Healing takes time. Give yourself grace and know that, one day, you will get there.

The biggest thing that helped me accept the grief and move on was when I sat on my porch and wrote the goodbye letter to Travis. Writing all the things that I loved and missed about him was my closure, my goodbye. It was like letting go of all the things I'd held onto for the past year — things I wasn't ready to acknowledge but knew were somewhere inside.

Ambiguous loss will remain with my family for the rest of our lives. But putting a name to the feeling has been very helpful in the journey. I know that I'm not alone, that many other people are experiencing the same thing. I also have a better understanding of why my mom and dad act the way they do. I am grateful that the letter I wrote to Travis was a closure for me. I'm not sure that either of my parents have found the same closure yet, but they are well on their way.

If you are trapped in ambiguous loss, feeling crazy like I did because it is an unexplainable loss, know you are not alone. Take a step back and look at how your parents or other loved ones are feeling. Which side of the spectrum are they on? When you have an understanding of what ambiguous loss is, you can work towards finding closure so that you can move on. Closure doesn't mean forgetting what happened or completely shutting people out of your life. Closure means looking at the events that took place and recognizing the feeling you have, *the loss*. Then do what you need to do to move on. Some have mock funerals to mourn the loss of the person their loved ones used to be. Some write goodbye letters like I did. It will take time, and the loss will always be there, but moving it out of the main focus of your life will help you move forward.

Relationships

"Only through our connectedness to others can we really
know and enhance the self. And only through working on the
self can we begin to enhance our connectedness to others."
– Harriet Lerner

Throughout my childhood, Travis was my best friend. We did everything together. Even through the early years of his substance use, we remained close. It wasn't until I moved out of the house at the age of eighteen that our relationship fell apart due to his substance abuse.

When Travis finally decided to get help and entered treatment, I wasn't eager to restart our relationship. I felt betrayed by him and wanted to move on with my life.

But he was persistent and continuously fought to prove to me that he had changed and was sober. The more time I spent with him, the more I began to trust him.

About three years into his recovery, we were basically attached at the hip. We lived close to each other, worked together, and spent most of our free time hanging out. Our relationship for the prior four years had been non-existent, so to have my old brother back felt amazing.

Because I was so happy to have my brother back, I felt that *all* the relationships in my life were good. My marriage was good, I had some girlfriends (although I didn't do much with them), and the relationship with my parents was in a good place. I felt content with where I was in my life.

I had no idea then that my relationships could get even better, and I could be even happier than what I was.

For so many years, I had wanted my family back together. When I finally had that, I held on to it for dear life. I felt like that was the best my life could get. I didn't need to have close relationships with my girlfriends because I was close with my brother. I didn't need to tell my husband all my deep dark secrets because I could tell them to my brother. In other words, my brother was the only person I, apparently, felt I could be vulnerable with. Why? I have no idea. Maybe I felt that way because I lost him once and, since he was back, would've done anything to keep that relationship.

I also wanted him to feel important in my life, so I spent a lot of time with him. Could there have been an unconscious fear that if I chose to do something with someone else over hanging out with him that he could relapse? Quite possibly.

I have spent a great deal of time thinking about the *why*. Why did I feel so content when my brother was sober? Why didn't I put any effort into other aspects of my life? Why weren't my other relationships as important? It's not like he was forcing me to hang out with him or threatening me.

I've come to the conclusion that I had no reason at the time to look beyond the one relationship, the relationship with my brother. I missed a chunk of my life growing up with him and, since I had him back, I really valued that relationship. I guess that could be true with any relationship. If you feel content, why look for more?

Then that relationship came to a halt. My worst fear came true: the monster Travis used to be came back, and I no longer had that relationship. My world was turned upside down. I was lost, I felt empty, and I didn't have anyone to lean on that would fully understand because I never let anyone else in. No one really *knew* me.

Yet the crazy thing is, as time continued to pass and the pain from the loss of our relationship started to fade, I started to see the other relationships in my life blossoming, reaching a level never in a million years thought could happen.

Let's start with the relationship with my husband, Ryan. We met while Travis was still using substances, and he was there for me when Travis went into treatment. Ryan and I have always had a good, open, honest relationship. When Travis came out of treatment, I was reluctant to get close to him again, but Ryan encouraged me. As I started to spend more time with Travis, partially due to the fact that we worked together, I kind of left my husband out. Travis and I had so many inside jokes that, when we got together as a family, Ryan had no idea what the heck we were talking about. I would say things like, "You would never understand," and not even try to explain it to him. If I saw something funny, I would text Travis. If something was wrong with my car, I'd call Travis. Travis was the person I would go to, not my husband. My whole life I've felt the need to be perfect, and Travis was the only person I allowed to see my flaws. I had this irrational fear that Ryan would leave me if I wasn't perfect. I felt that Travis would never judge me or ever leave me.

Of course, this was not intentional because Ryan is a fantastic man. If you would have told me at the time that I was doing this, I probably would have told you that you were crazy. I'm not even sure that Ryan even noticed. He never said anything, and, even since Travis's relapse, he's wanted me to try to get my relationship back with Travis.

But now that I'm two years removed from the relationship with Travis, I can see what I did to my husband. I wasn't vulnerable with him like I should have been. I wasn't as supportive as I could have been.

Now that I've opened up with him, our relationship has gone to the next level. Has he always looked at me like I'm the only woman he sees? How did I not notice that before? My poor husband. It's taken me thirteen years to be fully vulnerable with him.

And while I can't change the past, I can move forward. My husband deserves 100% of me. He's seen my flaws, he knows I'm not perfect, and he's always stuck by my side. He deserves the same in return from me. The need to be perfect stems from my childhood, and I've worked really hard to overcome it. Could he leave me? Sure. But at least now I feel that I am giving him everything I have because, damn it, he deserves it.

When the five-year relationship with my high school boyfriend ended, I had no friends. So when I met Ryan, his friend's girlfriends and wives adopted me. For the past thirteen years, we girls have been through many life stages: getting married, having our children, buying homes, and working real jobs. As most relationships do, we go through our spurts where we get together a lot and then don't see or speak to each other for months.

I will be the first one to admit I've never been good at girlfriend relationships. I don't go out of my way to check in on them or ask them to do anything. Life is hectic with three small children and I prefer not to add anything else on my plate.

Over the past two years, my girlfriends have been reappearing in my life. One girlfriend, Amanda, asked me to be a co-leader for Girl Scouts with her. My friend, Trish, and I made plans for a date night with a group of friends. The more time I spend with these ladies, the more time I want to spend. I keep asking myself *why* I didn't put in effort to maintain these relationships.

Although I will probably never have a clear-cut answer to my whys, I am thankful for the friendships I do have now. Going forward, I am going to do what I can to maintain them. It is possible to have multiple, fulfilling relationships at the same time.

When Travis and Cindy were together, Cindy and I spent a lot of time together. I would say we had a pretty good relationship. When they split, I took my brother's side and never asked questions. I took what he said about her as truth.

For so long, Travis had painted this picture that she was an awful person. So once I told her about Travis's relapse, I wasn't sure what was going to happen. I wasn't sure, after she left my house that day, if I would ever see her again. But quite the opposite happened.

We didn't jump into a best-friends-forever relationship right away. We made contact every couple of weeks to get the kids together. As time went on, we started to spend more time together and started to develop a new relationship. When either of us were struggling with Travis's relapse or anything that followed, we'd reach out to each knowing that we knew what the other person was going through.

We are at a point now where I say to people, "I may have lost a brother, but I have gained a sister." My relationship with Cindy is in no way, shape, or form replacing the relationship with my brother. I made a very conscious effort to make sure I was not swapping one for the other. Our relationship has built up slowly for the past two years. It's genuine and honest. And my kids *love* her, which is an added bonus. I honestly can't picture my life without her in it.

If I ever do have a relationship with Travis in the future, I believe I will still maintain my relationship with Cindy, regardless of what he thinks. In my mind, it's not an either/or. I have room in my heart for both.

The relationship I have with my parents has also grown. I've always been close with my parents. During Travis's recovery, our family felt complete with defined roles.

When Travis relapsed, we floundered. My mom and I didn't have a mother-daughter relationship because she was grieving the loss of her son and had no capacity to be a mother to *me* to help me with my pain.

Through many, many, many counseling sessions, my mother and I have been able to overcome those obstacles. Our wonderful counselor has said she has seen such a change in our relationship over the past two years. Although I cannot pinpoint what the change is, I do feel like our relationship is different.

When I think about it now, the one person I was the most vulnerable with hurt me the most. So, naturally, you would think I would be scared to be vulnerable again. But, for me, it had the opposite effect. I was vulnerable, got hurt, and, as much as it did hurt, I was okay. So if I am vulnerable in my other relationships and they hurt me, I will be okay. I know I will make it through.

Looking back on where my relationships were and where they are now has been an eye-opening experience. None of these relationship awakenings were noticeable at first, and I did not put a conscious effort into changing them. It all happened very gradually. Maybe it happened because I finally relaxed, opened up, and let other people in. However it came about, I am so thankful for them today. If I would not have lost my relationship with Travis, I would never have known there was more. I would have stayed in my place of content. As I've said and will continue to say, I wish Travis did not relapse. But, since he did, I am grateful that I have the opportunity to experience deep, meaningful relationships

My advice? Don't put all your eggs in one basket. Whether your sibling or loved one is sober or not, don't make them the only deep relationship you have. Make time for the other people who have been there for you to support you through all the crazy things life has thrown at you.

And, as hard as it may seem, it's okay to be vulnerable. The definition of vulnerable is: "Susceptible to physical or emotional attack or harm."[7] Being vulnerable is what brings you closer to people. If they hurt you, walk away, but know that you will be okay.

Take a real deep look at the relationships in your life, and think about how to make them better. You don't need a million friends; quality is better than quantity. I can tell you from experience, having more than one deep connection is possible. And boy, does it feel good.

7 The Free Dictionary, s.v. "vulnerable," accessed October 23, 2021, https://vocapp.com/dictionary/en/en/susceptible+to+physical+or+emotional+attack+or+harm.

Overshadowed Happiness

"Don't let others ruin your happiness just
because they can't find their own."
— Elle Sommer

In March 2020, I had lunch with my mom, Kasen, Cindy, and my family to celebrate Kasen's birthday. We had a great lunch, and everyone enjoyed each other's company, as usual. After lunch, we decided to take the kids to see my grandmother who had just moved into a new senior living center. We hadn't seen her in months because the facility she was living at previously had super tight COVID protocols.

Of course, Grandma was *so happy*! She hadn't seen or touched a family member in over a year. Even though this was such a happy and exciting time, in the back of my mind, I was thinking, *Oh boy, are we going to hear about this from my brother,* because Kasen was seeing my grandma on his mother's time. Travis's stance has been that if Kasen sees any family members on his side while he is with his mother, it's bad for Kasen's mental health. We know this thought process is absolutely not true and even verified it with a child psychologist.

That night, I sent a text to my mom and Cindy saying what a great time I had at lunch and Grandma's and that I hoped no one would get the wrath of Travis. I also prayed that Travis wouldn't take out his anger on Grandma or his son.

As I reflected back on that situation, I started to notice that our happiness can be overshadowed with worry or fear. It's sad when something as simple as seeing Grandma could potentially end up hurting someone innocent. It's also sad that we even have to feel that way. It's kind of a "damned if you do, damned if you don't" type of situation. On one hand, the fear of Travis's wrath could have prevented Kasen from seeing his great-grandma that day. On the other, Grandma could have received the wrath from Travis for Kasen coming for a visit on his mom's time.

I think this is something that a lot of us go through when dealing with a loved one's addiction. When I look back to when Travis was younger and using, I can pinpoint times in my life when my or someone else's happiness was overshadowed. Take my bachelorette party, for example. As I mentioned in Part One, Travis ended up getting arrested that night. It ruined my mom's fun and subsequently mine. My wedding is another example. I didn't know if he was even going to show.

This feeling was even present when he was sober. Six years into Travis's sobriety, Christmastime started to become a challenge. We never knew what mood he would be in, if he and his wife were fighting, or if they would even show. Maybe this was our past trauma resurfacing from his substance-using days, or maybe it was because he was drinking, but we didn't know. We just knew that the joy of Christmas was lost because everyone tensed up when Travis and Karen would walk in the house.

The first Christmas after Travis's relapse was tough. We were all scared that we would cry and miss him and his family. We knew that we didn't want to ruin Christmas for my children, so we decided to start new traditions. We ended up having the most relaxed and enjoyable Christmas we've had in a long time.

I wish it could end on that note, but it didn't. That happiness was overshadowed the next day when Travis called our grandma and yelled at her that he had no family and we were horrible people. As you can imagine, this deeply hurt my grandma. She didn't know what was going on because, quite frankly, we didn't

144

want to burden her with it. Travis also texted our mom half a dozen times asking where his children's presents were. She didn't respond.

When people talk about the rollercoaster of addiction, that Christmas provided an example. One minute we're happy, celebrating Christmas, the next minute, we're dealing with the consequences of having that nice Christmas. Next Christmas, this episode will be on everyone's mind. It's hard to be happy and carefree when people in your life feel hurt by your actions, even when you have done nothing wrong.

Looking back at the situation now, I think that, when my brother got sober and our family was whole, I shut everyone around me out. Nothing is more important to me than my family, and with Travis, it was almost like we were making up for lost time. When we were younger, we never spent time as a family, and now that we were grown and healthy, I wanted to spend as much time with my brother and parents as possible. We would laugh, make fun of each other, and just really enjoyed being together.

After a few years, this died down a bit, but I still put my family over every other relationship I had. My happiness was contingent on other people's happiness. If you would have told me this while I was in the middle of it, I would have laughed at you. Now that I'm two years removed, I see how much I missed out on life because I put everyone else's happiness before my own, afraid of the repercussions if I didn't.

As time goes on, my parents and I are becoming less and less worried about how Travis would feel. Yes, there are still times when I think to myself, *If Travis finds out, he probably won't like this.* Then I have to remind myself that I'm no longer living in his shadow. I am trying to live my best life no matter what repercussions may follow. When things do happen, I have to brush them off, understanding that his anger is *his* anger and there is nothing I can do about it. But I will definitely say something if he takes his anger out on someone innocent.

If this is happening to you, hang in there! Remember, don't react, *respond*. The more you react, the more they will continue to overshadow your happiness. Do what you feel is right, and let them deal with their emotions. At the end of the day, the only thing you can control is you and your happiness.

Tough Days

"The pain you feel today is the strength you feel tomorrow. For every challenge encountered there is opportunity for growth."
— Unknown

Finding your way out of the shadows isn't always easy. When you make the decision to let go and move on, it's not all rainbows and butterflies. Some days are awesome and you feel like you are on top of the world. Other days, you feel like everything just happened yesterday. Even two years into my journey, I have days that all I want to do is cry. Maybe I'm sad because I miss him. Maybe I'm sad because my kids don't get to grow up with an uncle. Maybe it's that I'm anticipating the next thing to happen. Or maybe I'm sad because the hope that things will get better is slowly fading away.

As my counselor always tells me, growth and healing are not vertical, they're circular. You're going to have good days and days where you can barely pull yourself out of bed. You have to give yourself grace.

Before this journey of healing, I always thought the bad days were a sign of weakness or a sign that I wasn't where I thought I was in my healing journey. I would say things to myself like, *Why are you crying? You should be past this already*. Or, *Seriously, it's been two years, move on already*. But knowing that this is part of the healing process gives me some relief. The self-defeating things I think about myself are just my insecurities.

So what do I do on the tough days when all I want to do is cry? I let myself cry. I allow myself to feel all the pain, hurt, shame, anger, and sadness. It might not feel great to feel all these awful feelings, but we have to in order to release them and move on. I think the fear of allowing ourselves to cry is that we'll never be able stop crying. But, trust me, you will be able to stop, and, when you do, you'll feel some relief.

When I get overwhelmed with the sadness, I sit in my favorite spot in my bedroom, or out on my porch, and let it all out. I bring my journal and, through my flowing tears, write my feelings. I feel like, if I put my feelings on paper, I'm sharing them with other people, and I feel less alone like somehow, someone can hear my pain through my writing.

At times, it's hard to share these tough days with other people. People who aren't going through this experience have a hard time understanding the pain. I can try to explain it to a friend, but I get these looks like, *That doesn't seem like a big deal, why are you so upset*?

My counselor said to me that the human brain brings past traumas to the forefront when something related happens. For example, if your sibling were to go missing for a few days, your mind would go back to all the times he went missing in the past, how you felt at the time, and the outcomes of those experiences. All those experiences come flooding back like they just happened. Then we feel like this thing that is happening right now is a major thing. But to people on the outside, it may seem like something minor. You may say to your friend, "Oh my gosh, no one has heard from my brother in two days!" And they look at you like you're crazy and say, "Maybe he's been busy." And then you get frustrated because they just don't understand. *They probably don't*. They don't have the flood of past experiences coming back. And if those past traumas have never been addressed, they'll come back even stronger.

I don't share this information to make you scared of tough days or to make you feel alone. You're not alone. But learning this information from my counselor really put it into perspective for me. Now when I do share things with people, I don't immediately jump to conclusions that they are dismissing me. I have to remind myself that my experiences are different from theirs and sometimes I need to provide additional context for them to really see the big picture.

It's even hard turning to my parents for comfort in times like these because they are living it too. They are already hurting, and I don't want to pile more pain on them.

Holidays seem to be the toughest for us. Not having a loved one at the festivities who has been celebrating with you for years can be tough. What's even harder is when they don't acknowledge you on your special days. Let me give you an example: Mother's Day. The first Mother's Day after Travis's relapse, Travis sat in the car while his wife and kids brought Mom a nice card and gifts. Why he sat in the car, who knows?

This past year's Mother's Day came and went with no acknowledgement from Travis. While Mom wasn't expecting anything, a simple "Happy Mother's Day" would have been nice. I realize that they haven't had a close relationship in almost two years, but she's still his mother — the mother that lied for him, stood in court and fought for him, and picked him up from a drug house in the middle of the night. She's also the one who visited him in treatment every day and asked every person she knew to send him cards. She was there when he struggled, cried, and wanted to give up everything. Now she's the one praying for him to get healthy, struggling to sleep, spending countless hours in therapy, and crying herself to sleep at night because she misses him. In the past thirty-three years of her life, she has done nothing but love him.

I can't quite figure out why Travis has so much hate for her. Is it because she won't go back to how things used to be, pretending like nothing happened? Or is it because she won't lie for him? Whatever the reason is, she is still his mother.

As a sibling, it's hard to watch. When the other sibling is not in the picture, they don't see the pain in their mother's eyes or hear the quiet sobs. They don't have to celebrate Mother's Day with their mom knowing that a piece of her is longing for her other child. We try to make up for it with funny jokes, nice presents, and good food, but it cannot fill the void. As hard as it is, we have to understand and accept that we will never fill that void no matter how hard we try. We must accept them and love them through the pain.

My advice: don't bottle it up, squash it, dismiss it, or repress it. On the tough days — holidays or not — feel the sadness, release it, and move on. The more we hold on to these feelings, the sicker we become. We end up having a short-temper and lashing out at people we love, or we get depressed. Find a nice quiet spot and *feel* it.

Finding Your Voice

"When you find your voice after so long…nothing, absolutely nothing, can silence you ever again."
– Phoenix Mode

For the past twenty or so years, I was voiceless. Nothing I said to anyone in my family ever mattered, so why even try? It was easier to stay in the shadows and keep my thoughts and opinions to myself.

When I was younger, I would try to speak up and share my thoughts, but I was always shut down because I was "just a kid." Sometimes, if I would say something, it would add even more stress and make matters worse. For instance, if I found out that Travis did something wrong, I would share it with my parents. Dad would be mad and yell and scream. Mom would cry. It was easier to not say anything just to keep the peace in the house.

I can see how that played out into my future relationships with other people. With my high school boyfriend, I just went along with everything he said because I had this fear, if I spoke up, he would leave me. After spending five years with him and then having some time apart from him, I found the courage to stand up and leave him for good. After that relationship, I vowed I would never lose my voice again, at least as far as dating relationships were concerned.

But I wasn't able to do that with my brother. Early on in his recovery, I thought, *He's just finding his way. You don't want to be the nagging sister.* So I wouldn't say anything when he did or said something inappropriate or disrespectful. I just let most things slide. As time went on, I guess I just adapted to not having a voice, accepting that's how it was going to be. In hindsight, that didn't do anything good for Travis.

As strange as this might sound, even to this day, I cannot pinpoint an exact situation where I should have used my voice. I can think of little things that were said but no major events. The memories must be buried too deep inside of me, or it just was so ingrained in my head that I shouldn't say anything, that they didn't even create a memory. But other people remember the events.

Katie once said to me, "You don't remember all the times he would yell at you for stupid stuff like missing a turn?" And honestly, I don't. She said she would sit in the backseat appalled by his behavior and shocked that I didn't say anything. But this is what I grew up with. Remember, I had this internal fear that he would relapse if I said anything and I would lose him again. I wanted my brother back so badly that I lost myself. Love truly *can* be blind.

When Travis relapsed, in the beginning, I was pretty silent. I was cautious of what I said or did because I didn't want him to turn it against me. I was paralyzed by indecision. I wanted to sit back and see how it played out, no matter what he said about me.

Once it was evident that the relationship between Travis and me was gone, I started standing up for myself. And let me tell you, he did not like it one bit. What I had previously envisioned would happen if I would say something — the thing that always kept me from saying anything — played out just like I thought. Only this time, I wasn't afraid of losing him because he was already gone. I was no longer afraid that he would yell, scream, or say hurtful things to me.

Going back to Part One of this book, I can pinpoint times I used my voice during his recent relapse: first was to tell Cindy of the relapse, second to tell him how I felt in a letter. Then I started calling him out on the bullshit lies he was telling people. I was no longer his compliant sister, hiding in the shadows, willing to play his games.

Finding my voice wasn't easy and was scary at first. I didn't know if he was going to retaliate. I was especially fearful when I told Cindy and we had our mini-intervention with him. Every time the dogs barked or there were strange noises at night, my heart would race thinking he was at my home. I don't think he's a violent person, but I'd just exposed his secret. He knew he could lose his son. At that point, I didn't know what he was capable of.

But as I continued to stand up for myself, I started to feel better. Early on, I was using silence when he would text, afraid of making things worse. But being silent always left me with the feeling that he figured he'd won. So instead of being silent, I started to respond. I responded in ways that he couldn't turn back on me. Because I had been working on myself, even though it was still early on in my journey, I knew that my response was more for me than for him. I made sure that any communication with him was clear and to the point.

Let me give you an example. When Travis confronted our grandma right after Christmas stating he had no family and making untrue accusations, I had to say something. What I really wanted to say was, *Grandma told me that you were yelling at her because you don't have any family and we're talking about you behind your back. You don't have a family because OF THE CHOICES YOU ARE MAKING. And no one is talking about you. So don't be a coward, leave our poor grandma, who knows nothing about the situation, alone. Man up and address your family.* Yet I knew that if I had texted him that and included emotion in it, it would have given him power. He would have gotten defensive and told me all the horrible things he thinks I am.

Instead, I texted him this:

"If you have an issue with me or think I'm talking bad about you, you are more than welcome to come to me directly. I've moved on with my life, and I have no problem discussing any lingering issues you still have with me. And I hope Maggie enjoyed the gifts the kids picked out for her."

He didn't respond. I felt that I kept my power in that text. My goal wasn't to shame him or make him feel bad. No, it was to let him know that I knew what was said and that he could talk to *me* about it. He had also made a huge deal about getting Kasen's Christmas presents from Mom, but never acknowledged the fact that we had given his daughter presents, so I included that in my text.

Finding your voice doesn't mean that you have to respond every time. There are things that have happened that I have just let go, and there are things that I *had* to say something about. If we respond to everything, then it just continues that cycle. I've always been cautious of how I respond because I don't want to make things worse for me, my parents, or even his son.

I asked my counselor how I should respond in certain situations. She advised me to respond with whatever is true and authentic to me. Don't say something I don't mean and don't lash out. I have learned from all the interactions that have taken place over the past two years that if I lash out in a way that shows he hurt me, he will keep driving the knife in deeper. This doesn't mean that I can't tell him how his actions made me feel. It means that I can't attack him about it. My responses have to be short, to the point, and 100 percent emotionless. If you look back at my example a few paragraphs above, you will see the difference in what I originally wanted to say (lashing out) and what I actually texted him (short, sweet and to the point).

One of the things we teach parents in the world of drug prevention is to remain calm. If they hear something they don't like or find something in their child's room that is not supposed to be there, we tell the parents not to overreact. Some people need ten minutes to cool down, others need a whole week. I have applied this rule to all my interactions with Travis. If he says or does something that bothers me, I revisit it twenty-four hours later to see if I am still bothered by it. Then I write down my response and give it another twenty-four hours to make sure that it's not me lashing out. Then I send it if I feel it necessary.

Having a voice has really helped me heal. Since I have been able to respond to the things that didn't sit right with me, I feel like I can let them go. If I don't say anything, the emotions spin circles in my head. It restarts that mental cycle of, *Why would he say that? How could he think that? I must be going crazy.* By being able to speak my truth, stand up for myself, and not spend countless hours looping in my mind about the situation, I've spared myself time — time that I can spend with my husband and kids, time that I can take for myself.

The longer I've been out of the shadows and the stronger I've gotten, the easier it has been to use my voice in all aspects of my life. My voice is not used to blame, shame, or provoke, rather it's used to help others grow. As I learned to do through the boundary work I completed, I try to provide *information that will be helpful to their soul.* Staying silent in the shadows helps no one. I still struggle with trying not to think that if I would have used my voice throughout all of Travis's recovery, we wouldn't be in this situation. Although I do know I can't blame myself for the choices he made.

If you are voiceless like I was, you got this. Start small, and remember to keep it simple. Once you start to use your voice, your healing journey will begin as long as you stay true and authentic to yourself.

Special People

"Special people — people we idolize, perceive as better, separating them from us." — Gabrielle Bernstein

Once Travis got sober the first time and started to rebuild his life, he gave off this confidence that people were drawn to. It was almost like, *Look at this guy, he was a down-in-the-dumps heroin addict, and he's rebuilding himself.*

Looking back, I think my family and I unknowingly put him on a pedestal. Eight months into his recovery, we started our non-profit, Your Choice to Live Inc. Our goal was to share our family story for others out there who were struggling with addiction so they would know they are not alone and there is hope.

The more we started speaking, the more people knew us. I think this really amped up the "special" attitude we all felt about Travis. Now I would say it was more of a *proud* special we felt versus a *superior* special.

But as time went on, I believe Travis started to think he was better than everyone else, or at least his actions made it seem like he did. And since none of us had boundaries and didn't want to put him in his place when he stepped out of line, it boosted his confidence, making him feel invincible.

I believe the "I'm special" mentality is one of the things that led to his relapse. In early recovery, every single accomplishment was celebrated. I remember when Travis completed his college courses to get his associate degree. My parents were excited like they had won the lottery. *Let's tell everyone, throw a big party, the world has to know!* Two years later, I completed my master's degree and…crickets. No one threw me a party, no one knew, no big deal. Did I say anything? No. I was used to it, still in the shadows. In truth, I was so proud of him that I didn't care about my own accomplishments.

As the years went on and things normalized, Travis became more equal to everyone. It was even coming to the point where he was no longer the "star" of Your Choice. More people wanted to hear the perspectives of those around the person who was using substances. We no longer needed him to function as an organization. I don't think he liked that very much.

Travis once told me that one of his biggest fears was that people didn't genuinely like him. When people stopped celebrating each accomplishment and he was needed less, I think, secretly, it hurt. By this time, his ego was so big that he would never share this hurt, not even with a counselor.

Looking back now, Travis always had a platform or this "special" mentality. When he was a teen and using substances, that was his platform: *Look at me, I'm a drug addict!* When he got sober, his platform switched: *I was a drug addict, but now I'm in recovery.* When he relapsed, he had no platform. I think part of him struggled with that. For so long, he was this "special" person who was in long-term recovery, even though he had been lying to everyone because he was drinking. Only he and a few people knew he was drinking. So when we found out about his drinking and took away his platform, he was angry.

He floundered for almost two years before finding his next platform: the victim. *I'm a thirty-three-year-old who has always been seen as a punk kid, dragged through the mud, brought to the depth of hell, and damn near broken to the point of no return.*

When I first learned about his new platform, I was shocked. For the past ten years, he'd relished in the fact that he was a punk kid that was now saving lives by telling his story of recovery.

People were in awe of him, proud of what he had accomplished. And no one was prouder of him than our family.

We started our non-profit as a family, and Travis played a big role in the development of the programs. He would take the stage at a high school auditorium and command the crowd. Eighteen hundred students were completely silent, hanging onto every single word he said. Students, parents, and teachers would all come up afterwards and share their stories of family members who struggled like him but were not as fortunate to find recovery, either passing away or still using substances. At one of our annual fundraisers, he stood in front of 200+ attendees, many of them lawyers, judges, law enforcement, or treatment providers, and told them that he had given them all a lot of money over the years and he'd like some of that money back. So when I found out about his new platform, I was shocked. It was completely the opposite of everything he'd been saying for the past ten years.

Now, I'm not saying that being in recovery is not a tremendous feat, because it certainly is. I'm proud of what he accomplished in the many years he was sober. But I think, for Travis's personality, the spotlight was too much for him.

By making Travis feel special and giving him the platform we did, we actually hurt Travis. I know it isn't our fault, and he would have found another platform, but it's hard not to wonder what would have happened to Travis if we'd never started Your Choice to Live Inc. Would he have gone on to work a normal job? Would he have stayed sober for ten-ish years? We thought that by sharing his story and being in the public eye, he'd hold himself to a higher standard, not wanting to let people down. But what would have happened to him? I know I will never know the answer to that question, but it's hard not to ask it.

My advice for any family with a loved one in recovery: be careful not to give into the "special person" mentality. Don't do or not do something because they seem better than you. Stay true to the person they are and the person you are. Any time you make someone special, you are separating them from everyone else.

Stuck Between a Rock and a Hard Place

> "Your worst battle is between what
> you know and what you feel."
> – Unknown

For me and my family, when Travis relapsed, there was the added challenge of being in the public eye. We had been open, honest, and real about sharing our experiences. What were we going to do now? Put him on blast for relapsing? Absolutely not. My mom and I continued to share our stories, however challenging it was. We even shared about his relapse. Your Choice was doing better than ever, and we were not going to stop doing what we were doing. In fact, his relapse showed how awful the disease of addiction can be.

In May of 2020, I was supposed to take part in a youth summit being put on by The Mark Wahlberg Youth Foundation. We were going to share our stories on stage with Mark's brother, Jim, in front of 4,000+ students. But, due to COVID-19, it was cancelled. Almost one year later and with a change of format, I was asked to share my story to be broadcast on prime time TV. Of course, I jumped at the chance. I was the first sibling perspective the foundation had ever had, and I wanted to make sure our voice was heard. It wasn't an opportunity I wanted to pass up.

But I also had some reservations. With the non-existent state of my relationship with my brother, I wasn't 100% sure what I could or couldn't say. When the interviewer asked me questions,

I stuck to the truth and never said one bad thing about him. My intention was to shed light on how siblings feel, so I focused on my feelings and thoughts and not just the relapse. After I was done answering questions with the anchor, the producer came on to talk to me. He had worked with my family on previous stories we'd done with this particular news station. He wanted to share with me that he was both shocked and saddened to hear of Travis's relapse.

The night that it aired, I was in Disney with my family. I was actually relieved that I was out of town because I didn't know how Travis would react. I remember sitting on the bus on the way to our resort and quickly hopping on Facebook to see if I could catch any of the show. I only caught the very beginning, but they were showing pictures of Travis and our family together and of Travis speaking on stage. I thought, *What the hell are they doing?* They were using all the footage they had from previous news stories with us. I didn't get to watch my segment until later that night, but they spun the story as the guy who found recovery but relapsed. I had absolutely no idea they were going to spin it that way. My segment was my interview with the anchor, literally five minutes on Zoom. After I had some time to think about how they aired the story, I was happy they did what they did. It really did shed light on how hard addiction is and that recovery is never guaranteed.

But I would be lying to you if I said I wasn't afraid of the repercussions that could possibly come from Travis. He had been fighting for over two years to keep his drinking a secret, even to the point of believing himself that it never actually happened. Then I went on prime time and told the world. Would he come to my house? What would his anger lead him to do? Would he sue me?

Nothing came of it — not a phone call, text, nothing — which I am extremely grateful for. But it put me in a difficult place: do I or don't I share what is really happening?

As we see with actors, singers, and anyone in the public eye, when you put yourself out there, everything shows. You can't only show the good side of yourself. The more I thought about it, I came to the conclusion that Travis can't bask in the glory of the success of Your Choice and then dismiss it when it doesn't fit his needs. He made his choice and marveled in the success for years, and rightfully so. But he can't just start being dishonest when it no longer works for him.

If I had pretended that he didn't relapse when I shared my story, I wouldn't have been my authentic self. *That* I could not live with. I had to be honest because that is what I am at my core, honest.

Even for people who are not in the public eye, I can see how this dilemma can be debilitating for families. If we share about our loved one's struggles, people will judge them and us. If we share about their sobriety, what will we do if they relapse? And if they *do* relapse, we don't want people to know because we don't want people judging them.

When we think about the stigma of addiction, this is the reality. You're damned if you do and damned if you don't. It's an added stress when we don't know what we can and can't say, and that keeps us silent. We don't feel like we can attend groups or reach out for help.

If we were able to have more conversations around the struggles of our loved ones, families wouldn't suffer all by themselves. Other people's actions, especially the people we love, deeply affect us. More people need to talk about it, not to shame or put down the other person, but to use their voice to say, *This choice this person made affected me in these ways. What are some ways that I can help cope with this situation?* Notice my statement was about *me*, not about the other person. You cannot control what they do or how they act, but you can control what *you* do. If we can have more conversations about how we can help ourselves instead of our loved ones, I feel like we would be stronger in difficult situations.

Every time I share my story, I have to relive the pain, hurt, anger, frustration, and sadness over and over. After the relapse, it would have been easy for me to throw in the towel and never talk about it again. Then I think of all the siblings I could help, the kids I could prevent from going down this path, and it makes it all worth it for me.

Hope

"Hope is being able to see that there is light
despite all of the darkness."
– Desmond Tutu

This book isn't about hope that your loved one will find recovery. It's about hope that, no matter what happens, *you* can be happy. Hope that when your world crashes down, you can pick up the pieces and rebuild. Hope that you can find your voice and yourself, and come out of the shadows.

I can sincerely say that I am the happiest I've ever been in my entire life. I never knew life could be like this. I thought that I was happy when my brother was sober but, now, I realize I wasn't. I wasn't as happy as I could have been. I am in no way, shape, or form glad that my brother relapsed. That, in and of itself, is tragic. Yet if that never would have happened, I never would have known this kind of happiness. I feel like he gave me the greatest gift he could have given me, the gift to be free — free from worrying about him relapsing. I think I, our parents, and everyone around him were so proud of him and his sobriety that we all carried this fear that he would relapse and we would never be happy again. Now that one of our biggest fears has happened, we no longer have to carry that burden. And Travis doesn't need to carry that burden either.

Through my painful, exciting, freeing journey of finding my way out of the shadows, I have learned a great deal. I have learned to set boundaries, forgive, and let go — not just with my brother, but with every other relationship I have. When Travis relapsed, I thought my life would be full of pain, regret, and loss. If I wouldn't have done the work that I did, it probably would be. Working on myself has not only helped me move on from the loss of my brother, but it's made me a better wife, mother, daughter, friend, and overall human being. Sometimes we have to do tough things, but those tough things come with great reward.

Epilogue

Where am I today? I am still very happily married to my husband, Ryan. This year, we are celebrating fourteen years of marriage. My three children, Nolan, Teagan, and Tenley, all have their own unique personalities and are thriving in everything they do. We live on a beautiful piece of land where we have chickens, horses, and a goat.

My relationships with my girlfriends continue to grow. In fact, for the first time ever, we took a girls' trip to Florida where we won't have to worry about children or husbands, or cook or clean for a whole weekend. We took a break from life.

Cindy and I are in a really good place. We can laugh and cry together about what has happened in the past, but we are able to move on and live the lives we deserve. I see my nephew all the time and am grateful that I made the decision to tell Cindy about Travis's drinking. If I hadn't made that decision, who knows where this story might have gone.

My mom is doing well. I am proud of the work she has done and where she is in her journey. We both have a better understanding of each other. While we might experience the same thing differently, we both have respect for how the other person chooses to respond. I would say that my mom is also the freest she has ever been in her entire life. She did the work and is also reaping the rewards. That's not to say that she doesn't still feel the loss of her son because she absolutely feels it every day. But she is able to recognize the pain, feel it, and move on. She's also learned to live in the moment and not worry about what is to come. She missed out on so many things in life because she was always worried about the future. Now that she lives in the moment, she is able to really experience life.

My dad — I'm not really sure where he is with everything. I think he's pushed the whole thing to the side and doesn't want to look at it. He's closed the book of Travis. This is, and always has been, his way of coping with problems. But that is his way of healing, and I respect that. Everyone is different. He has met with our counselor a handful of times, which has definitely helped him. I may never know how he really feels.

Throughout this journey, I have no regrets. I believe that everything I have said and done has been true and authentic to me. I know that my journey is far from over. And I know that the work needs to continue. There will be more disappointments, fights, and heartaches, but as I continue to work on myself, I will continue to be able to move past them.

Any day, I could get the call that my brother has passed away. I'm at peace with that. I know in my heart that every single thing I did for him along this journey was to help him get better, to help him grow. He may never forgive me for telling Cindy, but that burden lies with him.

If he ever wants to have a relationship with me, I am open to it. But I can guarantee it will be a lot different relationship from what I had with him in the past. I didn't do all this work just to throw it away because he wants a relationship with me. If he never wants a relationship with me ever again, I am also okay with that. We will cross these bridges as they come.

Although my work has been in the drug and alcohol prevention field for the last twelve years, I have a new passion for it. When we started Your Choice, it was to offer hope that a loved one can recover and prevent other families from living the nightmare we did. Now, my passion is to show those who are living through it that, no matter what the outcome is, you can and will survive. The work is hard and painful, but once you get out of the shadows, there is a whole new life waiting for you.

You got this. You can do this. I believe in you.

Bibliography

"6 Common Family Roles in an Addicted Household." Drug Rehab Options. American Addiction Centers, November 4, 2019. https://rehabs.com/blog/6-common-family-roles-in-an-addicted-household/.

Boss, Pauline. 2000. *Ambiguous Loss: Learning to Live with Unresolved Grief.* London: Harvard University Press.

Cloud, Henry and John Townsend. 2017. *Boundaries Updated and Expanded Edition: When to Say Yes, How to Say No To Take Control of Your Life,* Enlarged, Grand Rapids, MI: Zondervan

McLeod, Pat, Tammy McLeod, and Cynthia Ruchti. 2019. *Hit Hard: One Family's Journey of Letting Go of What Was —and Learning to Live Well with What Is,* Carol Stream, IL: Tyndale Momentum.

Ashleigh Nowakowski was born in 1984 in southeastern Wisconsin. Growing up with a sibling who struggled with substances created a home environment that was less than ideal.

Once her brother found recovery, Ashleigh, along with her parents, created Your Choice to Live Inc., a non-profit organization specializing in drug and alcohol prevention education.

For more than a decade, Ashleigh has been speaking in middle and high schools educating parents, teachers, and community members, and working with high-risk youth. Ashleigh is the voice of many who are silently suffering through their siblings' addiction.

Ashleigh has a Master of Public Administration, a prevention specialist certification, and is working towards her substance abuse counselor certificate.